WHY A POSITIVE ATTITUDE IS

All You Need

BY MATTHEW OGIEVA

Published at **DragonStar Publishing**
by Matthew Ogieva

ISBN: 1532705964

ISBN13: 9781532705960

Dedication

I dedicate this book to my friend and source…
God Almighty!!!

Author's Acknowledgements

I would like to express my gratitude to my mum Elizabeth Ogieva who taught me to read at a relatively early age, my late dad Sunday Ogieva who instilled the culture to read – without which I wouldn't be who I am today – and a pen in my hand and told me to always write whatever come into my mind on a paper as well as my late brother Ken Ogieva who always encouraged me to think differently.

I would like to thank my friend and source for enabling me to publish this book. Above all I want to thank my wife, Zino and the rest of my family, who supported and encouraged me in spite of all the time it took me away from them. It was a long and difficult journey for them.

How can I forget to thank Chris Obanga of blessed memory? Who was the first person to take any of my work through typesetting and have it printed decades ago; that experience gave me that piece ownership. He was a huge fan and an immense encouragement.

Thanks to Genevieve Flight and her team for

putting in the Midas touch - without you this book wouldn't be this good.

Last but not the least, I beg forgiveness of all those who have been with me over the course of the years and whose names I have failed to mention.

Foreword

When I travel around the World to attend Conferences, Meetings, Events or deliver a presentation, I always get to meet people who have succeeded in various life goals. One thing exciting about these class of people is that they are always ready  to help others towards achieving their goals and subsequently helping to change the face of the World among all those they come in contact with. This is where Matthew belongs.

———

In this book, Matthew will be taking you through a very comprehensive look into 'Why A Positive Attitude Is All You Need' to succeed exceptionally well in diverse areas of life while passing through the challenges and many lessons that life presents before us.

In essence, it is a reminder that our attitude to everything in general is all related to our psychological, mental, emotional, educational, spiritual and social values which on the other hand are all influenced subconsciously by our beliefs or limiting beliefs.

Matthew also reminded us in this book/ebook about the 12 Key Universal Laws and how deeply our energy vibration and frequency could either be working in harmony or disharmony with these Laws of Nature, thereby shaping our everyday life experiences.

These are some of those hidden mysteries that we need to be mindful of if we do really wish to grow and rise higher above the challenges of this life.

Matthew has done justice to this book/ebook and I am sure you will enjoy reading it from beginning to the end.

Genevieve Flight
Life Coach/Spiritual Coach/Healer/Author
@Genevieveflight
London, United Kingdom

CONTENTS

Introduction

Attitude = Altitude

Have you had the opportunity to work with an individual who is gifted, proficient and qualified, but still never appears to excel? A large portion of us have sooner or later. On the other hand, have you met somebody not exactly as gifted, but rather appears to dependably be excelling at all angles?

The contrast between these two kinds is not exactly their intensity of aptitude or information or proficiency. It boils down to one single issue; Attitude.

If you are a Team Leader, a Client Manager or a Support Staff Member, the intensity of achievement you will attain is reliant upon one criterion; your Attitude.

Your disposition - your methodology, perspective or supposition (whichever you lean toward) impacts the way you perceive everything close to you - your part, your undertakings, your objectives, your associates, your present circumstance and your future plans. Basically, your state of mind is an amalgamation of your practices, convictions and sentiments, your encounters, training and identity defines your attitude.

Been privy to this, it turns out to be moderately

simple to see why a few individuals are effective and others are definitely not. It has to do with their state of mind and attitude.

Consider what characterizes a positive state of mind in your business:

- ❖ A general "can do" perspective on your part can take away the difficulties.

- ❖ Readiness to go the additional mile to assist a customer or take care of an issue is always helpful.

- ❖ Persistence in managing complex problems is important.

- ❖ Seeing issues as a way that will help you learn and progress should be welcomed.

- ❖ Giving recognition where it is expected, by acknowledging the endeavours of your associates and expressing gratitude toward them openly is ideal.

- ❖ Search for opportunities, not crisis.

- ❖ Disregard habitual pettiness and simply embark on dealing with the issue.

- ❖ Recognize and grasp distinctive perspectives.

- ❖ Understand that being correct at other people's expense is not the right way to teamwork.

- ❖ Be calm, considerate and practical in the way you deal with problems.

- ❖ Although this is one part of the many attributes of an uplifting disposition, you may start to understand that an associate who shows these practices is an unbelievably much needed resource in a business.

On the off chance that you have an uplifting attitude, you are prone to:

❖ Be flexible and rapidly recuperate from obnoxious or troublesome circumstances. You will search for lessons in the occurrence as opposed to ceaselessly thinking back on how awful it was.

❖ Be hopeful about what's to come. This positive thinking will go a long way to help people close to you.

❖ Be sure about your capability and capacity. You will see areas of advancement and improvement and cheerfully grasp the learning.

❖ Assist you to deal with your feelings and express them in useful ways

❖ Assume liability for your activities

❖ Imagination outside the box and contemplate all alternatives, even the ones that seem far-fetched.

❖ Essentially, your disposition will predict your level in business and life. An uplifting disposition towards your employment and your objectives can be the determinant of your prosperity. That is, a hopeful standpoint can do methodology and perspective that anything is conceivable; will regularly furnish you with the vitality and excitement to be successful.

❖ Does Your Life Feel Like Out Of Control?

Does it appear to be something or another person who is responsible for your life? On the off chance that you suspect as much, you may be correct! The issue with such a large number of individuals today is that they have either been modified with or have built up a negative mental state of mind. Truth be told, what you have gotten to be and where you are currently in your life can easily be followed back to an initial source: the decisions you made as an aftereffect of your ruling contemplations and attitude.

As such, if your life seems like a runaway train, there is a justifiable cause. The contemplations that have swirled around inside your brain have at last emerged all things considered, framing the particulars of the life you are currently encountering. Basically, on the off chance that you have a negative mental state of mind, you can't create a fantastic life.

The vast majority are caught up with attempting to either change their circumstances or other individuals to make their life more agreeable and compensating. Be that as it may, the issue is inside. You may obtain a University degree; encompass yourself with powerful companions; or appreciate a renowned family name.

Yet, in the event that your brain is loaded with negative thoughts and a defective state of mind, those accomplishments or favourable circumstances won't deliver the achievement and satisfaction you crave.

It may be of assistance to reflect about your psyche or mind as the software in a PC. In the event that your software or psyche is brimming with uncertainty, dread, and indecision then, regardless of how hard you attempt, you will simply create an item or an existence that repeats those negative convictions. As such, in the event that I scrutinize your life in close proximity, I have an inconceivably precise idea of what you have been considering.

I am certain we all have heard stories concerning individuals who experienced childhood under alluring circumstances; some may even have been mishandled or relinquished. But they figured out how to succeed, to place themselves in the record book in numerous occasions. What actions did they take? They put themselves through a complete state of mind upgrade! They changed the information in their 'life programming' built up an I-will-not-be-denied-demeanour and, subsequently, they created an alternate life.

When I was a young fellow, I grew up supposing I possessed a decent state of mind which in real truth was an awful one that about pulverized me. My disposition dragged me toward a different sort of life which wasn't a perfect one. In any case, I just declined to be demoralized, debilitated, or devastated and that is the reason I needed to decide to change the state of mind keeping in mind the end goal was to be a superior individual.

Accordingly, after some time, the external aspect of my life aligned with the internal.

It's dependent upon you to make the move to change your thinking, your state of mind. You don't need to be controlled by the words that may have been said around you as a toddler, or by words you constantly repeat over yourself.

You can begin now by being attentive to the contemplations that swirl in your psyche and inevitably leave your mouth. When you utter words out of uncertainty, trepidation, and cynicism, you harvest an existence that shows only that. What you think about turns into your utterances, and your utterances turn into the moves you make, and the moves you make decide your life.

Achievers are continually searching for approaches to end up more fruitful; to achieve objectives all the more rapidly and with more prominent affirmation.

Also, for a considerable length of time, creators have been sharing the elements that help anybody achieve their objectives.

On the off chance that you consider accomplishment and achievers, you ideally would perceive that one bit of the objective accomplishment riddle is mentality.

In most objective accomplishment compositions I`ve read, attitude is constantly talked about, frequently made light of and normally misjudged in the whole objective accomplishment riddle.

Three great reasons to investigate the 'right` state of mind

I will list what the correct attitude to support objective accomplishment is, and why it is imperative to us as people and pioneers and how to create it.

Consider the three P`s of the right goal achievement Attitude:

Positive

It is the place the majority of these discussions begin... furthermore, ends. Winning astuteness and much research demonstrates that having an uplifting attitude enhances the probability that you will accomplish your objective, hastens your advancement and, maybe in particular, makes you stronger - majority of which assists you to overcome obstructions and stay steady in quest for your objective.

Possibility

The way to plausibility is conviction. Do you trust you

can succeed and achieve the objective? Do you trust we can win it? Do you trust the objective is conceivable? On the off chance that you think it is workable for others; would you be able to see it for yourself? It is more than a mere augmentation of positive consideration. All things considered, on the off chance that you didn't think the objective was achievable, how likely would you say you are prone to accomplish it?

Proactive

The correct disposition isn`t regarding speculation and conviction alone. The right disposition incorporates understanding that you must get off from your seat and do something. As you make a move toward your objectives, you can assemble force, more noteworthy conviction and improve your mentality as you go.

The majority of this resonates really great, I understand, however what makes this the "right" disposition; or, all the more basically, how does this demeanour aid the circumstance?

The right state of mind empowers the right practices - practices of constancy, order and inventiveness.

The right state of mind empowers right motivation - keeping focused target and awareness for circumstances.

The right state of mind empowers right results - it enhances the probability of your achievement in coming to your objectives.

Practices, motivation and results. The right demeanour can make every one of them, both for us and those who follow.

You understand what the appropriate demeanour looks like and you understand it is more than 'simply' positive mental attitude as it identifies with objective accomplishment, you may be considering how you would make it. That's another incredible investigation. Here are some important steps:

1. Set the objective

This is the beginning. Prior to accomplishing an objective you need to recognize what it is. This gets everything under way. The nature and size of the objective will affect each of the three P`s portrayed previously.

2. Include the individuals who will be accomplishing the objective-

If you need others to have confidence in the objective, you must include them however much as could reasonably be expected. The right state of mind comes simpler when members possess the objective.

3. Make more noteworthy conviction

Remind individuals of past triumphs; compensate and commemorate little victories on the accomplishment way. As you do this, you make a forceful impact and the more prominent conviction floats the mentality.

4. Get energized for the objective

Truly this is misquoted. Don`t concentrate on the objective itself, get yourself as well as other people energized for the advantages that originate from accomplishing the objective. When you privy as to why you are undertaking the (difficult) exercise of moving toward an objective, you are making the right attitude.

5. Make the objectives visual and striking

Assist individuals to "see" the accomplishment of the

objective. Although this has as of now been said, it is basic. Assist your group make that image as genuine as possible. At that point, at whatever point conceivable, assist individuals to remember that vision.

6. Keep the objective before you at all times

Do you have a list of your objectives that you study regularly? Do you have group objectives "recorded" or outwardly accessible to individuals in numerous places?

Do you create group events by assisting individuals to remember their goals and objectives? When we are assisted to remember the objectives of what we wish to accomplish, we will always wish to remain focused mentally in order to achieve it as desired.

We all understand the right mentality will have any kind of effect. Presently, you know a few reasons why, and how you can impact and support that state of mind in yourself, and those who follow you. When you get the mentality right, you are quickly sending your advancement towards accomplishing your objectives.

Pioneers realize that to be fruitful, they must accomplish objectives and help other people do likewise.

Chapter 1

Developing a
Positive Mindset

Having the capacity to stay positive when things aren't working in your favour is what characterizes the quality of your ethical values and your definitive joy. An incredible state of mind means feeling hopeful in troublesome times. Remember your good fortune.

Search for the silver lining in everything and be thankful for the things you have. Simply concentrating on the immense things effectively introduced in your life prevents you from concentrating on what's inadequate. In any case, what else would you be able to do to keep up a positive attitude?

Here are six straightforward yet successful approaches to making and keeping up a positive outlook, particularly through troublesome times:

Decide to be Enthusiastic

Think excitedly. Speak enthusiastically. Get to be enthusiastic by acting energetic. Your positive attitude, contemplations and practices set up your eagerness. Drive yourself to act with eagerness, and soon you will feel excited.

Be lively

Walk rapidly. Put a skip in your stride. A fiery, generous handshake proposes you are happy to be alive and upbeat to be with other individuals. An inviting grin emanates intrigue and attracts others. Individuals will need to associate with you.

Discuss great things

No one ever earned a companion or achieved anything important by passing on awful news. Uplifting news, be that as it may, advances positive attitude spreads eagerness. Continuously strive to make the individual you converse with feel superior to anything they generally would. Keep negative remarks and tattle out of your discussions.

Conceive your craved results

The best entertainers imagine achievement. Before you choose to do practically anything, close your eyes and envision yourself executing it perfectly.

Converse with Yourself

What were your utterances to yourself today? On the other hand yesterday? Then again a week ago? Did you groan concerning others? Did you imagine negative contemplations? What we believe is 100% determined by our feelings. On the off chance that our contemplations are reliably negative, our activities will also be negative.

Like being around others, bring consolation, energy, and joy to everybody you come across. Assist other individuals feel welcome around you. Spread satisfaction and goodwill.

Be worried about the aspirations of other individuals. Be mindful, understanding, forgiving and tolerating. Turn out to be more worried about helping other people accomplish their individual yearnings.

By beginning with these straightforward approaches to enhancing your reasoning, and adding to a positive attitude, you can be far on your goals to attaining the progress you need.

For a large number of us, we are so caught up with concentrating on the negative that we all the time self-destruct ourselves. We have to comprehend the force of our brains.

Is your thinking preventing you from accomplishing all that you cherish in life?

Step by step instructions to build up the right attitude & Develop Self-Esteem

It may appear to be extraordinary, yet the individuals who create the right outlook in life always succeed at whatever they are determined to achieve. Have confidence in yourself, and have positive mind-sets. They will have the capacity to achieve their objectives in life, and overcome deterrents that may try to stop them.

The individuals who have negative mindsets will abandon all endeavours towards their objectives. Most will quit imagining. They will kick back and reassure themselves that, "I can't accomplish it". They will lose the fight without even trying to mount a challenge.

There are numerous strategies to use and build up the right attitude that will overcome impediments that may keep you down. It may take a sometime to master, yet the individuals who set aside the time to attempt, discover that they will get to be fruitful at anything they need to do.

1. Get up in the morning with a Smile

Do not consider what took place yesterday that may have brought on some torments. Keep in mind that today is a fresh, brand new day and a new chapter, so put aside every negative thoughts and channel your energy on the positive.

2. Start the day with purpose and not with apprehension

Normally, every day begins as an obscurity for the individuals who have no particular arrangements. Take it step by step. Realize that anything should be possible for those who need to do it, and that they can spend the day in any capacity they please.

The individuals who work ought to attempt to make the workday wonderful. Be decent, amiable and supportive to the individuals who strive with you. Create positive considerations, and don't think back to the torments of yesterday.

3. Prior to climbing into bed at night

Take a couple of minutes to bless the day. Be

appreciative for your excellent wellbeing, being financially buoyant, and having the funds to purchase your necessities. The individuals who use their skills should be grateful that they have an occupation. Add inspirational demeanour to great things in life and build up the right mentality to fulfil whatever it is that you set out to accomplish.

4. Be mindful of your environment

When you come across somebody lounging alone on a recreation centre seat, looking tragic and discouraged, you ought to make proper acquaintance and after that continue strolling. This may be the sole individual that had conversed with you all day.

Make proper acquaintance with those you come across in the market, if the time is proper. Try not to appear, by all accounts, to be pushy as a well mannered "howdy" will suffice. Being polite and kind to others can make anybody feel useful for whatever is remaining of that day. Additionally set aside time to favour others.

5. Build up the right outlook and discover some new information

Do what you generally needed to do yet never have the chance, cash or craving. Those whose occupation is indoors can figure out how to become a bird watcher. The individuals who are confined to seats throughout the day at work ought to begin taking strolls.

Join the Mall Walkers and make new companions with the individuals who likewise walk. Join a recreation centre to lose a couple pounds if you are obese, or despondent with your appearance. Realizing that they appear great to others will make them feel satisfied with themselves.

The greater part of us have a thought regarding what achievement is to us, and we have a mental vision of what it will look like when it touches base in our lives.

We may at long last get the job acknowledgment we've been working hard for, receive a considerable amount of cash, discover the man or lady we had always wanted in life for a loving relationship.

We could start a family, buy our own home, purchase the dream car we've craved since we were young, or achieve any number of other individual achievements. Is this achievement? For a few of us, it may be. Maybe you have an alternate vision of what achievement is to you.

Notwithstanding your own meaning of progress, you likely possess something in the same manner as whatever remains of us. You are as yet looking for the level of progress you need to accomplish. Possibly you've had accomplishments in specific areas, yet not in others.

Your vocation may be going awesomely; however, your connections are deficient. Then again, you've met the love of your life; however, you just can't get the cash that would make you comfortable. Then again, everything else is awesome; however, you can't lose those last 20 pounds and show signs of improvement in shape.

It's an irritating position to be caught in, particularly in the event that you don't comprehend why it's happening. You may believe you're doing everything correctly, except that circumstances just won't cave in to your will. You always keep running into deterrents, that undermine your own particular endeavour. While you do not blame yourself for your disappointments, the battle continues.

This battle continues on the account of one purpose, and one reason; just that you are putting your energy and strength in the wrong place.

In recent times, we have the misinformed idea that achievement is some slippery quality "out there" that we have to chase down and catch. We trust that on the off chance that we say the right things, do the right things make precisely the right calls, achievement will fly directly into our little butterfly net and we can bind it on a sheet of cardboard and hang it gladly on our wall.

We can't catch achievement, nor would we be able to purchase it, unearth it, or fall into it. We can just create it, from the beginning to the end. What's more, the best way to make it is by changing our frequency, considerations and propensities. What role dose contemplations play in anything? Everything! We see only that which we want to see. What we hope to have in our lives, we have. What we concentrate on the most and put our energy into grows and expands.

On the off chance that your life isn't what you crave, your contemplations have not been in line with it. This can be a dubious idea to see, however the most vital point to get is that it's an aggregate procedure.

Imagine a scale. On the off chance that you put a grain of sand in one of the plate, it presumably won't have much effect to the scale's equalization. In any case, if you include an extra grain, and another, and another, a little while later the scale will start to tilt in towards the weight. Your contemplations work similarly, and in the event that you have enough of one specific sort of thought, it will influence your personal satisfaction.

This may sound terrible, yet it's really something to be thankful for! In the event that we can make awkwardness and need with our contemplations and propensities, we can likewise make wealth and accomplishment with our considerations and propensities. Everything is exactly within our grasp.

Imagine a scenario in which I let you know that just by altering your thinking; you could start to easily draw in the achievement you want. Imagine a scenario where you couldn't just pull in achievement, yet get to be fruitful at a centre level.

You definitely can! By taking after the certain demonstrated methods, you will figure out how to change your reasoning procedures and add to genuine progress thinking. What's more, with the right personality set, no restriction exists to what you can make of your life. The vital thing to recollect as you set out upon this excursion is that it's a procedure.

Alter your Mindset & make headway

It is safe to say that you are discharging your mind, to create room for achievement? Having the right mentality, is the distinction between being poverty-stricken and being well off. I will demonstrate to you generally accepted methods to change your outlook, discharge your negative considerations and substitute them with positive contemplations.

Permitting change in your life can be more difficult than you might suspect. To begin with you've got the opportunity to perceive that you have to change your mentality. Much the same as a dependence on medications or liquor the first attempt toward recuperation is to admit to the issue.

"I am poverty-stricken and have been a pauper for the greater part of my adult life, regardless of what business or project I attempt to do in order to get wealthy, I generally end up becoming broke. I am here today to recoup from my limiting convictions and dependency on poor mentality."

Would you be able to say the expression above, perhaps you have to adjust it to your own circumstance, however say it with conviction so we can advance to the second plan of your recuperation to change your thinking.

Since you've acknowledged your optimum mentality has gotten you so far today, how about we discharge your mind and alter your thinking.

To begin you require an objective, something to centre your psyche, an extreme objective for achievement. You have to see the end of the tunnel. The tunnel can be rough with numerous snags and you have to come out the opposite end.

Give me a chance to clarify. I am an incredible devotee to representation and that implies that you have to see and touch what you need to accomplish. On the off chance that you identify with effective individuals, they have seen and felt their prosperity before it took place.

The most effortless approach to bring out this inclination and imagine it is via music. Music has a propensity for blending up recollections and feelings from deep inside. That enthusiastic feeling you get, when you hear certain tunes, is the thing that you have to feel. That inclination is the thing that you have to feel when imagining your prosperity to help alter your mentality.

Here's a method that can assist in changing your mentality and helping you imagine what you need to accomplish. Adjust this activity to fit in with your intended vision for accomplishment.

Either replay the song again or listen to one tune

that stirs up affectionate recollections. Shut your eyes and let the music wash over you and stir those sweet feelings we smother in our regular lives.

Immediately you've caught that feeling envision yourself in that fantasy house, playing your desired tune. While in your fantasy home, imagine your furniture, kitchen, what painting plans you have made. Would you be able to inhale the aroma of your choice dish originating from the kitchen? Go into subtle element, see and smell everything, experience that moment.

To alter your attitude, you have to change your negative contemplations and inquiries, with positive answers.

What if I fail? - I'm not certain I can achieve this. - If I fail to make a move, then I won't end up a failure.

Apprehension of disappointment can be a genuine test. Think about the open doors you've missed previously, due to your trepidation. Diminish your apprehension, by assembling a Plan B, what are your choices; make tentative strides, little objectives prompting your definitive objective.

Simply make a move, be assured, you will even amaze yourself. There is no such thing as disappointment, simply new encounters to gain from and enhance yourself for your next test. Stay on it, there is a chance for development. They are lessons of life.

What will individuals think of me?

These are the pessimistic considerations that have pulled you backwards, and will keep on holding you in place, on the off chance that you don't dismiss them. You have to answer every one of these inquiries decidedly.

You ought to understand, that people are very narrow minded and self retentive. Individuals don't generally think about anybody other than themselves. So you shouldn't mind other people's inclinations. You will acquire regard, by taking after your own particular way to achievement and not the well used out regular way that keeps more than 95% of the populace poor. Be the decision effective 5% by being distinctive.

To alter your attitude, you have to remain engaged and connected to, with standard positive certifications. This will keep you on track, to accomplish that protected rich way of life you have imagined.

The most effective method to use and enhance your self-esteem

Whatever transpires with you is an impression of what you accept about yourself. We can't beat our level of self-regard. We can't attract to ourselves more than we might suspect we are worth."

One trademark normal for achievement is high self regard. A solid feeling of self is discriminating keeping in mind the end goal to explore life. How is your self regard? Does it require a support? How would you go about enhancing it? Enhancing you regard starts with legit self assessment. In the event that you need assistance evaluating the wellbeing of yourself regard, you may need to address specialists that are proficient in the field.

Why Self Esteem is important

The strength of your self regard is imperative on the grounds that it decides a massive part of who you are and how you associate with the world. It has an impact on your mental prosperity. Self regard is your general perspective of yourself, particularly in respect to others. Said another way, it is your general view of self and your apparent worth as a person.

It is conceivable to have a high self regard in few areas of life and yet observe minor self regard for others.

A 40 year old lady, for instance, may have to a great degree high supposition of her value as the bookkeeper or mother or Author. These backgrounds fill her with fulfilment and she is sure of her skill in these parts of her life. In the meantime, she may be experiencing little self regard as to her self-perception which makes looking for garments, getting dressed and mingling particularly hard for her.

At the point when poor self regard is constrained to a couple of unmistakable ranges of life, it as a rule is less demanding to distinguish and right the restricting conviction that is at the base of this negative self discernment. On the off chance that there is a general feeling of poor self-esteem, be that as it may, a considerable measure more escalated exertion is expected to redress the conviction framework behind this for the most part negative mental self view.

Your Belief System and its relationship to Self Esteem

Your conviction framework, manufactured through innumerable one of a kind backgrounds since conception, is the foundation of yourself regard. A solid conviction framework corresponds to a sound self regard. Each idea, how you feel, react and each choice you decide are always being sifted through your one of a kind conviction framework and are essentially educated by it.

Markers of High Self Esteem

You for the most part relate well to others
You are confident
You possess a high level of key qualities and rules that you abide by
You are aspiring
You consider yourself worth, significant
You have a cheerful attitude
You cherish yourself
You have self regard
You heed your gut feelings and oppose control
You feel cable
You brim with self assurance
You feel intriguing and meriting extraordinary companionships
You feel delightful

Markers of Low Self Esteem

You feel unstable about your place on the planet
You stay away from difficulties at work or social exercises
You feel unworthy, second rate
You are unsure, on edge
You are extremely touchy to criticism
You are extremely self discriminating
You are uncertain
You feel pitiful or demoralized
You feel embarrassed
You harp on past slip-ups
You don't relate well to others
You feel jealous

You feel that the world is out of line

You treat yourself inadequately and permit others to treat you severely

You suck up to people and frequently acknowledge short of what you merit

You think everybody looks preferable and dresses better than you do

You are exorbitantly poor and clingy

10 Steps to Improve Your Self Esteem

1. Read books or materials on the subject of self help and put recommendations into practice.

2. Look for the assistance of a specialist or therapist if self improvement is insufficient

3. Keep an everyday diary of your self-refuting considerations. Substitute each with something positive.

4. Use this diary to help yourself to remember your achievements and your best qualities

5. In the event that self-perception is an issue, look for expert help to build up a get-healthy plan you can hold fast to.

6. Surround yourself with constructive individuals, positive books, and positive music

7. Take in another aptitude or enhance one you have as of now. It has been demonstrated that individuals who get to be fruitful at something see change in their certainty and self recognition.

8. Enhance your physical appearance through activity or an individual makeover.

Studies demonstrate that when you look extraordinary, yourself observation makes waves. It is additionally genuine that the world reacts to you contrastingly taking into account your physical appearance.

9. Recognize parts of your life where you are typically a sucker and make an arrangement to end up more emphatic in those zones.

10. Make plans to be cheerful about the great things throughout your life.

Vision for Your Life

In the event that you have a fantasy that you have postponed on the grounds that you don't feel sufficient or sufficiently commendable, a sound help of self regard may be everything you need with a specific end goal to alter your life.

A solid self regard can engage you to think better, turn out to be more certain, accomplish all the more, live all the more energetically and even accomplish the impossible. This month, focus on making your life a study in merit - starting with yourself regard.

Chapter 2

Channeling Positive Beliefs – You Are What You Think

Your Thoughts make things

Your contemplations make the things in your life, starting with the substance world you possess, to the body you reside within, to the stage of wellbeing you get the chance to appreciate, to the connections you have and even the otherworldly decisions you choose.

Wouldn't you say that something, which can shape everything as far as you can tell, to be specific your contemplations, ought to get some uncommon consideration? You can no more permit them to simply haphazardly drift through your psyche, similar to a bit of wood gliding heedlessly around on the sea.

The time has come to intentionally arrange your contemplations by making an arrangement of rules for guiding them later on.

What are these rules?

The rules I am alluding to are a clear vision statement, which is composed, effectively comprehended and rehashed frequently all day. When you comprehend where you need your life to go later on and you back this image with an arrangement of nitty gritty key arrangements, you have the capacity to arrange your thinking, which will thus drive you to make the day by day decisions.

Predictable, coordinated contemplations, which guide you to make the right objective particular move every day, will dependably bring about greater accomplishment.

It all begins with a Thought

All that you see around you today was initially CONCEIVED in somebody's creative ability and after that with steady BELIEF and a dosage of day by day steadfast activity; they turned a basic electrical charge in their brain, into something genuine and substantial.

You can also change your thinking into something genuine and substantial, by believing that you are ready and capable to take on and practice the basic rule depicted above, when you have some decisions to make with the goal in mind that understanding its application will help you to make the right objective decision every day.

Have bigger prospects

It requires as much vitality to make an immense arrangement of objectives as it does to make an exceptionally constrained idea, which does not stress you by any means. Are your imaginations and desires in accordance with what you are really fit for accomplishing or would you say you are holding so as to sell short yourself onto those little, sub-standard dreams and objectives?

Do you make HUGE assumptions about everything? Do you hope against hope? Do you have any motivating dreams? The bigger your desires, the more prominent will be the result or results you can achieve later on. You will never surpass your own desires, so quit undermining your capabilities with little indistinct dreams and set out to see awesome opportunities as you grow mentally, psychological, educationally, spiritually etc.

Live life, be innovative and have tremendous EXPECTATIONS. It is those exceptional desires that will motivate you to stretch out yourself and drive you to accomplish your maximum capacity.

Constrained desires will convey restricted results, whilst HUGE desires will convey the outcomes you merit. You really are grand and equipped with a mentality which is loaded with arranged thoughts, which push you to take the right steps every day, you can accomplish anything.

Choose your Thoughts Wisely

Wisely decide on your thoughts and make progress toward greatness as consistently as possible. Ask yourself if this is the best way to spend my time. At whatever point you feel that you are not using your time effectively, quickly distinguish and use a more beneficial approach towards your time and adjust your choices as needs arises.

You can turn into a super achiever in the event that

you use your thoughts to create the right every day activities and you use your time adequately.

Use your Time Wisely

Until you quit exhausting your vitality on the little stuff, you will not have space to make the truly critical things work for you. Find that one thing that will aid you take a transient step toward your prosperity and afterward apply steady and industrious exertion every day until it is finished.

Every single super achiever knows the worth of prioritizing. Channel your strength on doing the right activities consistently and achievement is conceivable, as well as unavoidable.

Go to the Future

Clarity of Thought and a detailed composition of Vision permit you to go see the future and see the prize, which anticipates you. When you know the guarantee tomorrow holds, it is far less demanding to pay the cost of predictable exertion today. This clarity of thought permits you to begin visualizing so as to practice your future in your NOW?

The more frequently you do this, the more auxiliary strain you make between your present reality and the magnificent future you have imagined. This basic strain will assist you to stay enlivened, notwithstanding when things get intense.

Continue Rehearsing your Future

No stage demonstration would ever be fruitful or a blockbuster without practice. On-screen characters invest hours doing things repeatedly until they can perfectly perform them.

When you apply this standard in your life, imagining yourself performing the objective particular activities you have to succeed consummately, you drastically build your possibility of making your future, precisely the way you need it to be.

Contribute the energy to arrange your contemplations, make a dream and an arrangement of point by point vital arrangements to guide you, make motivated steps day by day, and imagine your future achievement in the now, and every plausibility gets to be accessible to you.

You now have the equation for opening your fantasies. Presently all that is needed is your dedication and a sound measurement of day by day control and you can have, do and be whatever you like. It's anything but difficult to tell an individuals' prevalent thoughts just by the way they live. Individuals who think absolutely appreciate an existence loaded with wealth, success and unlimited potential outcomes. Their vitality, through intuition positive contemplations, has a gradually expanding influence on anybody within their vicinity.

Thinking is Energy! When we consider something, we send that Energy out into the Universe, and the Universe will give that Energy back to us. On the off chance that the Energy you sent out is negative in nature, then you can see that negative recurrence will keep coming back to you in same structure.

What are your first thoughts when you get up in the morning?

In the event that your foremost thought is:

"Gracious, another exhausting day at work"

"There's insufficient time to do everything"
"I detest my career"
"I don't like my appearance"

By concentrating on considerations like these, particularly when you first wake up, you're setting the tone for your day.

Be that as it may, in the event that you think effective, positive contemplations in the morning, such as:

"Much thanks to you for this excellent day"
"I'm going to finish so much today"
"I cherish the way I look, and I adore myself"
"I cherish my occupation and my colleagues"

You will harvest the prizes by beginning your day with an inspirational demeanour. Record some positive attestations that will fortify a more positive state of mind.

Discuss them every day and you'll be amazed what amount more vitality you'll have. In a matter of moments, you're going to notice that individuals around you will stick around a bit longer as a result of that radiant vitality.

Have you ever seen that there's dependably a man at a gathering that individuals appear to incline toward? Everybody calls them the "life of the gathering". That individual most likely spotlight on satisfaction, affection and plenitude and that intensely positive vitality reflects in the atmosphere or vitality around them.

Individuals are pulled in to that inspiring vitality like flies on nectar and actually they need to be near that individual. Concentrate on what you posses, be grateful for it, and figure out how to adore yourself. Think magnificently constructive thoughts and see as individuals notice and begin staying close to you more often.

With so much apprehension and tension on the planet at this moment, everybody can profit by pausing a minute to themselves to concentrate internal, to where our actual quality and strength dwell.

Every one of the impediments we've overcome in the past make up how we turn out today. Concentrating on the present with a feeling of appreciation and certainty will establish the framework for a copious future.

Could The Power Of Positive Thinking Really Change Your Outlook On Life?

While everyone has likely known about the term positive mindset, not everyone trusts it is something that can be use effectively. A large portion of the individuals who are cynic about positive intuition force have never taken a stab at utilizing it, so they simply don't see exactly how fruitful it can be nor do they see how intense positive deduction is. Positive thinking alone can change your whole point of view thus significantly more, on the off chance that it is used accurately.

A best aspect concerning positive deduction being sufficiently intense to alter your point of view is how many different things throughout your life will be altered with it.

Individuals who kick back and concentrate on the adverse parts of life are frequently pessimistic individuals; they are not exceptionally enjoyable to be around. All things considered, you most likely have a couple of colleagues that are continually being negative, saying something isn't possible.

These individuals let themselves know frequently enough that things aren't possible, so they have persuaded themselves that it is difficult to achieve.

Something else intriguing to note about constructive masterminds is that they are the ones that individuals constantly need to be close to. In the event that you consider this, it presumably sounds good to you as of now.

No one needs to be around the selfish individuals, yet everyone needs to associate with constructive, positive minded and goal orientated individuals.

The major motivation behind why constructive individuals are so enjoyable to be around is that they are constantly cheerful and in an energetic disposition.

These temperaments really rub off on other individuals and give them a great feeling, which is the reason such a large number of individuals like to encompass themselves with constructive intuitive individuals. So to use positive energy to change your point of view you need to begin applying it in your daily activities, as well as the need to surround yourself with other positive scholars.

Keeping in mind the end goal is to start utilizing positive intuition to change your point of view you should figure out how to use it successfully. Many individuals accept that everything about using positive thoughts is letting you know a couple of positive words every day.

In any case, and to use positive intuition to its utmost best, there are a couple of different things that you have to complete. Positive intuition is more than simply letting yourself know that things will be fine, it is likewise about your state of mind.

A standout amongst the most vital things to do

when using positive deduction is to just use positive words. This applies to your thoughts, as well as any words spoken that anyone might hear.

You need to keep away from the greater part of the negative words, for example, can't, won't, not ready to, and so on. Rather, concentrate on the positive words that make it appear as though anything is conceivable. Case in point as opposed to saying "I am not certain I can do something", say "I can do this".

In the event that you locate a negative thought coming in, which is conceivable regardless of the fact that you are trying your utmost best, you basically need to divert your line of consideration, sort of like that old saying "turn that frown upside down."

Before you embark on doing something, regardless of how little the assignment may be, you will need to set aside the time to envision what it is you will be doing. At the point when imagining the arrangement you need to envision one that has a fruitful result; don't consider any sort of disappointment. Focusing on the result that you need and having confidence that you can make that result happen is the best thing you can do to guarantee your triumph.

In addition, above all you need to be in the midst of other constructive individuals, additionally other positive things. Case in point, rather than watching films that make you feel pitiful or irate, watch movies that make you glad.

Reading motivational books is another tremendous stride to changing your point of view, yet you can likewise read different books that make you upbeat. Simply verify you are reading one page of a persuasive book every day to help surge your brain with those positive and cheerful considerations.

Since you know how to use positive thinking adequately, you have to ensure that you are doing it well. You are not going to have the capacity to effectively change your point of view essentially by spending a couple of minutes every day letting yourself know that things will be alright, you need to put some time and vitality into this procedure keeping in mind the end goal is to triumph. So why are you hesitating, go out there and begin.

Do Thoughts influence Your Reality?

What truly influences our world? Is it our mindset or feeling?

On the off chance that you have listened, watched the motion picture or read the book titled 'The Secret ', you will realize that basically you can show your wishes by employing the Law of Attraction for what you need, trusting that it is conceivable and expect that it will occur.

In any case, is this enough? The firm answer is NO. To make your sought after reality, you have to not just see or imagine yourself living your dreams however, you likewise need to feel the sensations you would have in your body as though you were really living that craving.

Competitors have been employing this strategy for a long time with extraordinary achievement.

Arnold Schwarzenegger used to sit in the seats at the spots he would be vying for weightlifting competitions and imagine himself up on the stage, doing his thing, listening to the gathering of people cheer, listening to the judges call him the victor, seeing himself being given the trophy, all the time feeling the feelings, the vitality, the delight, the triumph of being called a champion.

He did this such a variety of times that he knew on the real day of the opposition, that he had effectively won the occasion before it even began in light of the fact that he had as of now been there both in mind and soul. And also won.

Tiger Woods additionally pictures and feels his golf wins. He sees himself heading off to each hole on the course, feels the wind and the temperature, sees and hears the multitude, feels the surface of the grass and the hardness of the ball, feels the power of the club as he hits the ball, watches it fly through the air and arrive on the green.

He too knows he has won the occasion before it has begun in light of the fact that he has officially played it over in mind and soul and triumphed.

With cutting edge innovation, first class competitors have been determined electronically to run their race in their brain. They envision strolling into the stadium, seeing and listening to the people, feeling the air temperature, situating themselves in the beginning lines, the firearm going off, the spectators thundering, opposing competitors running next to them then crossing the finish line having won.

When they review the outcomes, researchers have possessed the capacity to demonstrate that the body has physically responded in the same path pretty much as though they had really run the race yet the entire time they were sitting in a seat and not running by any means - astounding isn't it. The reason that representation and feeling the sensations works is on the grounds that our psyche can't perceive between what is genuine and what is envisioned.

So the stunning effortlessness of this is that in the event that you envision your craving in subtle element and feel the body impressions of that imagination, your psyche will be persuaded that you are really living that yearning and by the Law of Attraction you will carry that longing into reality. You did! You can imagine.

As I have said some time recently, it's not simply the perception; it's likewise, vitally, the sentiment of your imagination. To help yourself, record in subtle element what it is that you need to make in your life. What is it, where is it, what does it resemble, what flavour, who is likewise there, what are you doing, how do you feeling.

Constantly placing yourself in the photo in a manner of speaking, all the more effectively you will have the ability to feel the circumstance you seek. You are hoping to encounter solid intense sentiments, not wishy washy ones. It is the power of your feelings that will achieve the indication of your yearning.

A glorious approach to realizing that you've 'got it' is the point at which you are imagining your longing, feeling the sensations and you all of a sudden understand that you are grinning and that you feel cheerful - that is the point at which you know you are intensely making your own particular reality.

As you will eventually come to discover, it's considerations that make our world, as well as our feelings and our emotions likewise assist in making our existence. It truly is an inclination universe.

Chapter 3

Use of Positive Words

Systems for Efficient Use of Positive Affirmations

On the off chance that there are any places throughout your life that you need to alter and enhance, you can boost the improvement or change happening all very effectively with positive affirmations.

Positive affirmations are effective constructive contemplations or messages that are instilled into the brain, particularly at the subliminal level, to help improve the most constructive environment in a man's mind.

They are currently very well known to be of benefit and are generally used by a lot of people. Here are some powerful and supportive strategies that you can attempt to make your attestations more compelling and more visible in your life.

1. Maintain short and straightforward affirmations

Positive affirmations are intense, so you don't generally need to make them hard or lengthy. Actually, affirmations must be kept short, basic, and straight to the point. Utilizing more confounded sentence structures can lessen the viability of positive affirmations.

2. Be privy to the top hours of positive confirmations

Affirmations likewise posses what could be called "top hours". These are the times of day when using affirmations is generally recommended. The top hours incorporate the time before you go to rest and the minute after you wake up. In both occasions, you are still and as of now unguarded, and you have a clearer head in those times than amidst your occupied days. Besides that, these top hours are better in light of the fact that positive assertions are most effective when the psyche is at its most loose state of mind.

3. Record your own voice

One extraordinary strategy in showing the positive outcomes of positive affirmations is consistency and reiteration. To make it less demanding for you to adhere to your attestations and say them all the time, it might be ideal in the event that you make your own recording of the listed affirmations you need to apply in your life.

As indicated by specialists, your own recordings may be more viable than the subliminal items that can be purchased around on the grounds that your psyche perceives your voice all the more effortlessly and along these lines will naturally believe in yourself.

4. Stand up and trust your affirmations

Do not simply hold back your affirmations to yourself alone. Make a point to get the word out so that the whole universe will likewise be altered in a positive manner. This will develop the healthiest environment for a more positive personality.

Along these lines, you won't be enticed to do a reversal to your old negative propensities in light of the fact that your surrounding is as of now transformed to continually drive positive messages into your head. Continuously seek after the affirmations with as much enthusiasm as you possibly can be able to.

You can likewise record them and make stickers so you can place them in key places where you can read them effortlessly.

5. Say them regularly

Do not let your down your guard when you embark on a positive affirmation venture. Consistently encourage your brain with these insistences. A brain that is continually assaulted with these affirmations will actually be more readily centred, and will consequently be more powerful in showing the affirmations throughout your life.

In any case, on the off chance that you don't say the affirmations constantly, you are allowing diversions to barge in on you and disillusion your mentality.

Chapter 4

Visualise Your Way to Success

Similar to an automobile, our brains are hot-wired to function in a particular manner. At the point when taking in another skill, such as playing an instrument, at first it may feel cumbersome strumming the strings or playing the notes, however as we keep on playing, our mind really shapes dendrites or pathways that make memory. Subsequently, the more we practice ability, the less demanding it gets. Before long it turns out to be second nature, we don't even need to ponder on it.

At the point when taking in another aptitude or positive propensity this frequently attempts further backing our good fortune as new errands will get to be less demanding and simpler.

Nonetheless, we can likewise master ruinous or unfortunate propensities that can conflict with us too, particularly regarding the matter of unlearning them.

Much the same as our brains retain our monotonous positive activities; it likewise remembers our negative ones, making it significantly more hard to modify.

These awful practices are ingrained into our minds or sub-cognizance and we frequently do them naturally and without any misgivings until sometime later. That is the point at which we get to be disheartened or nauseated with ourselves and ask, "Why do I continue doing this, despite the fact that I try not to?"

A major approach to check or alter negative practices or negative thoughts is to picture yourself acting differently or how you for the most part respond or by making another decision different from your normal, reoccurring practices.

How about we use nourishment as a case. You may have a propensity for eating inadequately around 4 p.m. regularly. You are very much aware of this and each morning you announce that today won't be same. You will fight the temptation to eat at 3 p.m. Well 4 p.m. arrives and the sensation to eat something surpasses you and the enticement is just too difficult to stand up to.

Then again perhaps you eat incredibly much when at home in light of the fact that you don't purchase garbage nourishment, yet have some major snags leaving behind the doughnuts in the staff lounge or at your companion's residence. The time to control this conduct is not when you are faced with the nourishment, but rather before the enticement emerges. Here's the method to adopt:

For the following few weeks and in any event twice per day, envision yourself saying no or declining when enticed to eat ineffectively and after that see yourself elated about not giving in.

Researchers say that the mind doesn't recognize

creative ability or perception from reality. It's much the same as contemplating a lemon can make your mouth water or considering a frightful wrongdoing can make you disgusted.

So every time you say no to enticement, even in your visualizations, you're assembling new thoughts or dendrites to bolster your new conduct.

In the matter of negative behaviour patterns, there are frequently triggers that draw out the most exceedingly terrible actions in us or our profoundly situated insecurities. It's useful likewise in the event that you can recognize the triggers, which will make you act rather than respond when they emerge.

For instance, ordinarily at 3 p.m. you may feel a vibe of fatigue and despair and crave food for solace. By been privy to your activators, you can use it as a piece of your perception to overcome particular actions.

Once more, employ your brain, creative ability, and imagination to make new endings to your negative behavioural patterns. Utilizing the above sample, during your 3-5 minute perception, imagine yourself being surpassed with fatigue and the craving to eat for solace, and after that envision the inward turmoil you may feel.

Next, imagine yourself saying no to the allurement or conversing with yourself, urging you not to give in. After that, envision yourself substituting the unfortunate propensity with something positive like going out for a stroll around the square or drinking a large cup of water. Do this a few times each day for the following couple of weeks to give your mind time to master your new demeanour?

You will notice that the imagination will pass on to your genuine reality, signifying, that when you start to feel pressured to get a treat, your cerebrum may go after the water or recommend going out for a stroll.

You can use perception to control numerous sorts of programmed reactions or passionate addictions like modesty, workaholic behaviour, overcoming outrage, Smoking and that's just the beginning.

I have sketched out the progressions below:

1. Understand the conduct you need to change.

2. Understand any activators that more often than not happen that incite the above conduct.

3. For 3-5 minutes start the perception by envisioning the conduct, activate, and the internal clash that emerges inside of you.

4. Envision picking an alternate reaction than ordinary or the exact opposite.

5. In your creative ability complete the new reaction or conduct.

6. Envision how great it feels to triumph. See others commending your achievement.

7. Repeat regularly.

Step by step instructions to envision achievement

As indicated by the word references, success is "the achievement of a point or reason; the accomplishment of acclaim, riches or societal position and the great or awful result of an endeavour". For a great many people, achievement implies some sort of blend between money related prosperity and accomplishing what they've embarked to do.

When you first begin a business, achievement is sure to be on your list of milestones you need to accomplish. In any case, sadly, when things get intense, it's just too simple to dismiss that achievement and what you were planning to accomplish. One sure method for keeping accomplishment in your cross-hairs is to have the capacity to imagine it.

Imagination, put essentially, is the ability to envision something and is a method used by a wide range of sports men or women; working class and effective individuals all through the world.

Once in a while depicted as somewhat of a hippy idea, solid proof of the adequacy of representation is difficult to bind, yet there is assurance that the demonstration is one which can assist individuals make a considerable measure of progress. There is a considerable measure to discuss in terms of perception however we've decided to concentrate on 5 activities to help you imagine your prosperity:

1. Characterize what achievement is to you

If you were to stop ten individuals on the road to ask them what achievement is to them, it's verging on certainty that you'd get ten unique answers. The meaning of progress differs from individual to individual and nobody can characterize what achievement means to you aside from you. It sounds obtrusively self-evident, yet it's completely vital before you attempt to picture your prosperity, you characterize it.

Accomplishment for you may mean the leeway of obligations; the accomplishment of a superior work: life adjustment; a sound speculation portfolio or basically internal peace.

However, keeping in mind the end goal is to picture that achievement it's crucial that you characterize it and characterize it unmistakably. Once you've characterized it in a worldwide sense, set to work to characterize the subtle element. Note down every one of the components of your prosperity and get a picture in your mind of how it will appear.

2. Choose how you're going to arrive

Only once you've characterized your prosperity would you be able to choose how you're going to accomplish it. It might be that you choose to establish a home based business which you can supervise around your occupation, which will permit you to acquire additional cash to pay off your bills.

It might be that you choose you will decide to work low maintenance and invest more energy with your family or you may settle on a totally distinctive lifestyle to make your progress, however in any case, you have to record plainly characterized, achievable strides to achieving your prosperity.

3. Characterize what your prosperity is going to resemble

When you characterize achievement and choose how you're going to arrive, you'll begin to get a mental picture of what your prosperity will resemble. Envision the individual you want to be when you achieve your aim.

Toward one side of the scale, it might be as straightforward a dream as snickering on the shoreline with your children or at the other; it may include budgetary issues like a performance automobile or a better house.

Regardless of how you characterize achievement, it's going to look different to what you see when you take a look at your life today. You are more inclined to make that progress on the off chance that you can build up a mental picture of what it will look like and store that mental picture in your mind so you can haul it out when hard times arise and let it help you get back on track.

4. Choose how you're going to quantify your prosperity

No matter what individuals let you know, overnight achievement is extremely uncommon. In light of that, it's crucial that once you've characterized your prosperity you set up quantifiable and identifiable points of reference for achieving it.

These developments will be of colossal aid to you on the off chance that you discover yourself straying from the success lane you've set for yourself. These developments will allow you to make any restorative move you have to get you back on track in the event that you've gone off and will obviously give you that important inspiration when you require it most.

5. Choose how you'll feel when you've finally triumphed

Success needn't be about outward showings of riches or bliss. Achievement is regularly basic about feeling better. Feeling better about the world; feeling better about your chances; feeling better about yourself.

Regardless of how withdrawn you are with your emotions, the procedure of envisioning achievement is an extraordinary approach to get back in contact with them.

Record how you're feeling today. How you're feeling about what you've accomplished: in your life; in the most recent month; in the most recent year, indeed over any period of time you like. It's your arrangement.

At that point, record how you envision you'll feel when you're fruitful. Attempt to truly stick into this one: toward the day's end, you burn through every day with your emotions, so getting them to where you need them to be will be an enormous accomplishment. An immense achievement!

Achieve your objective by perception

Now you have put in place some effective objectives and you have a technique to work towards accomplishing them. What else would you be able to do to guarantee that the objectives you have figured are met viably and as indicated by your schedule? And also looking into those objectives routinely and changing them as vital, I would firmly recommend that an essential device will be perception.

You have set aside time to record your objectives in a manner that 'the other than cognizant personality' is willing to acknowledge. By making this stride you have effectively begun to reconstruct your psyche, adjusting it to that which you will draw in. Day by day perception will drive the process of reinventing your life in forward direction. Well how is it achieved? It may take a touch of practice, tolerance and self-control like whatever else is beneficial; however it soon turns into a programmed ability. It additionally turns out to be more charming after some time, particularly as you turn out to be more innovative with it.

Let's make an illustration. You may have an objective for your financial accounts which may be:-

'I have no less than 200,000 in my financial balance by 28th August 2015'

Close your eyes and breathe deeply. Take a few steady breaths.

Visualize yourself reading your bank balance. See the exchanges and the sums. Take a look at the balance.

See yourself opening the mail and discovering large money cheques with your name on them. Yes, visualize your name and the sums written on the cheques. Picture, browsing the web and seeing the statements to your account balance increasing enormously.

Picture what you are putting on. After every one of your funds has maximized significantly, so in your perception, do you possess a designer suit? Have you purchased some extravagant jewellery for yourself?

Use your different faculties as well. What are individuals saying regarding your recently discovered riches? Your spouse definitely would have some incredible things to say, as would your family members, companions, neighbours and business partners. What are the discussions you are presently having with your bank chief?

Maybe there are smells and tastes included. You may be welcome to ceremonies by wealthy personalities. Envision then what the dishes and beverage will savour like. Notice the feel of the cheques and the vibe of your new garments. The greater amount of your faculties you can include in your perception, the better. Continue trying, bringing more detail into your imaginations and making it all greater and clearer. Imagine in colours. Watch the scenes as though they were a motion picture, with you being the director and main performer. You can envision it how you need it to be.

Maybe in particular, envision with feeling. It is this

that adds fuel to the perception. The subliminal personality can't recognize reality, and something which is envisioned, particularly when the feelings are included.

The sample I gave you was for the range of funds, yet it can be connected to some other objective you have as a top priority. Take wellbeing for example. See your body as an exceptionally sound body and feel the general wellbeing all through your body every last time you consider your body.

Furthermore, I am going to present a picture mystery that will skyrocket your showing abilities out of the stratosphere. Go to the automobile showroom and test-drive that top of the list vehicle that you have had your eye on. Take in each part of the experience, the odour of the calfskin, the smoothness of the drive, the ideal sound of the stereo framework, the vibe of the rigging stick, grip and brake pedals.

Drive with feeling as though the vehicle was at that point yours. This will obviously add substance to your day by day perceptions. This can be connected to anything. Request to be taken around a property that is available, which you can envision owning and living in. Converse with an organization about that fantasy position that you strive for. The more fun you make your perception the more effective it will be for you.

Chapter 5

The Importance of Taking Positive Actions

Possessing the Right Mindset can alter the outcome of Your Efforts

The right personality set, particularly of the way you consider yourself, can have numerous outcomes in the consequences of your endeavours. Those that obtain positive contemplations and can apply that sense to their lives and endeavours may additionally get the best results.

It's a common truth that your contemplations control what you draw in, whether negative or positive. It's a basic idea known as the "Law of Attraction". In the event that you can ace this law of attraction, the potential outcomes are unfathomable. Entryways that have been shut by resistance will open without exertion.

You must trust that you possess what it takes to accomplish your objective. Napoleon Hill, writer of

"Think and Grow Rich", built up a self authority in this subject and has been cited in his book to say "What the brain can consider and trust, it can accomplish."

The achievement of all business people that have gone well beyond to accomplish and get their objectives has been an aggregate aftereffect of having confidence in themselves and NEVER surrendering. Envision yourself as officially coming to your objectives and life has a baffling effect, also called the Law of Attraction, of turning them to reality.

Presently, I have an question for you, are you a fence straddler or a fence jumper? The distinction is whether you can settle on a fast choice or not when you are confronted with an open door. The capacity to continue getting up and go and not be weighed down by hesitation can have the effect in the middle of achievement and disappointment. Most new business people get stuck in "examination loss of motion" and get to be baffled at the way that they simply don't appear to be getting any closer to achieving their objectives.

At the point when a chance presents itself before you, do your investigation and settle on a choice. Once the choice is made, don't squander your vitality on stressing in the event that it was a decent choice or not, it's called taking risks. Also, odds are what we do every single day unknowingly.

From driving, to looking for the right item or administration, to choosing what nourishments to consume and so on. These are all choices we make every day and we are taking risks at all of them.

We have no real way to know precisely what the result will be in each choice we make, so when offered a chance to roll out a major improvement in our lives, why do some still delay? It is simply about Confidence!

Having trust in you is one of the vital achievement to a business person. Having the capacity to walk tall without trepidation or uncertainty about what others think or say as regards to you decides your level of accomplishment in anything you put your brain to.

One of the greatest dream stealer in life is having inadequate conviction and certainty expected to do what it takes to be the individual you need to be or execute the things you've for a long while been itching to do. Nobody, regardless of who they are, were they come from, what foundation they possess, ought to feel mediocre compared to any other person's prosperity level.

We are all the same and all have the same measure of time in a day as those with an exceptionally high state of achievement. So absence of fearlessness ought not to exist in an existence of wealth, where there is abundance to go around for everybody.

Another part of learning to have the right personality set is to set sensible desires and hold yourself at risk to those fleeting objectives. Unlikely objectives can make a man question whether the real objective is achievable. Try not to lose the certainty and centre in your endeavours to achieve your objective by committing this error.

In the event that, for instance, your objective is to earn $50,000, don't use a date that clearly is improbable unless you have set a positive arrangement of activity in which you accept can be accomplished. Rather, make the sum coincide with the set period of time.

That way it is more achievable and inspiration won't be lost if the particular objective is not achieved. You can simply set a later date for the same objective and proceed with your endeavours in acquiring that objective. The key here is to keep on moving toward your desire with vigour and never stopping. Above all, have some good times.

In case you're boring yourself while working at coming to those desires, you will lose inspiration and your endeavours will simply appear to be stressful. That is the considerable thing about the day and age we live in.

We can influence innovation to help secure new companions and business accomplices if the time to physically perform this activity is incomprehensible. I've by and by made more companions and business associates through the utilization of Internet social platforms than I've ever done in person. It simply gets difficult to physically be all over at the same time.

Having made these marvellous companions gives me the fundamental positive surrounding to concentrate on my objectives and continue advancing in life.

Whether it is individual or through the utilization of innovation, appreciates the experience of meeting new individuals and making new companions. Doing as such keeps your psyche set laser focused, engaged, spurred, and certain that what you need from life you will achieve.

Chapter 6

The Negative Influence of Limiting Beliefs, Fears & Worries

Our most profound apprehension is not that we are deficient. Our most profound trepidation is that we are intensely unimaginable. It is our light, not our darkness that most terrifies us. We ask ourselves, "Why should I be intelligent, lovely, skilled, and awesome?" Actually, who are you not to be? - Marianne Williams

It is regularly said that state of mind is the best indicator of achievement. How genuine... how genuine! It extremely well could be that nothing is more critical than your state of mind. Truth be told, as I would like to think, for you to understand your most prominent potential and productivity, you must have the right attitude.

If you lack it, the chances of fulfilling your objectives are lower than they ought to be. I would prefer not to get into the mental parts of this, however our convictions about what we can achieve, what we are deserving of fulfilling, and the amount of cash we ought to make are established in the profound openings of our psyches.

A few individuals call this self-talk, i.e. letting ourselves know - intentionally or subliminally - that we do or don't merit a particular thing... that we can or can't accomplish an objective... that we are or are sufficiently bad.

Be that as it may, to make progress, you need to realize what you need, why you need it, how you are going to accomplish it, and why you merit it. Anything less places pointless impediments in your path. Who wants that?

There are as of now enough deterrents to maintaining a fruitful business. You would prefer not to include more. Indeed, even the best experience the ill effects of this pain.

You don't need to be a world-famous artist to scrutinize your legitimacy.

A large number of us grow up imagining that a high level of accomplishment, anyway you characterize that, is for other individuals - that we ought to be fulfilled by "bringing home the bacon."

If this is the thing that you truly need, that is fine. In any case, a significant number of us could profit, have all the more leisure time, and have less cerebral pains by working for another person.

As I see it, on the other hand, in the event that you need to function as hard and as constantly as you need to, you should be effective. Why would it be a good idea for someone to else to merit it instead of you?

The awful news is that every one of us - of all shapes and sizes, youthful and old, rich or poor has some level of self-talk or negative mentality that impedes our advancement at some time.

The uplifting news is that you can defeat it. Figure out what it is that you do to destroy your prosperity. Self-doubt, negative intuition, procrastination or impeding mentality is only a couple of the things that could be hurting you. Search for even the scarcest occasion of these or different difficulties. When you get to be mindful of them, do all that is important to defeat them.

Burrow profoundly inside of yourself. What do you do that keeps you away from coming to your definitive objectives? In what capacity would you be able to change your state of mind? In what capacity would you be able to be as fruitful as you have permitted yourself to imagine? Choose to set your objectives and make progress and don't let anything keep you down... not even you.

Negative mentality can possibly devastate your life. A psyche that is loaded with negative thoughts can make one vibe troubled, hopeless, and can prompt many disasters, regardless of how hard one strives to succeed.

On the off chance that you have mastered a way of negative thinking, you are more prone to be the particular case that will wind up with poor connections, dangerous ones, furthermore be under water. Along these lines, if you truly need to make it in life, carry on with an existence of thriving and plenitude. To appreciate genuine satisfaction, you are going to need to take out the negative convictions that you hold.

You're going to need to substitute those negative convictions with positive ones that can permit you to carry on with the sort of life that you truly need to live.

Despite the fact that it might be somewhat difficult, it's more straightforward than you might suspect.

Here are a couple of approaches to take out negative thinking and make the life you had always wanted. Most importantly, we should backtrack to the point of view.

How do negative contemplations begin in any case? All things considered, we need to understand that we all have negative considerations and, as hard as we attempt, we are not ready to dispose of every one of them.

In any case, on the off chance that we get rid of the unending ones, the ones that keep repeating themselves again and again, can help us change the course of our lives. Anyway, the question is: What are these unending thoughts and where do they originate from?

These unending thoughts originate from our companions, wife, spouse, accomplices, our guardians, our kin, our colleagues, educators, even from outsiders, and above all they originate from us, from right within us. You know, it's difficult to acknowledge, however it's true.

We make the greater part of those contemplations. As you most likely are aware, we thoroughly consider 60,000 contemplations a day, and from those 60,000 thoughts, we just recall a couple of them, and it's simply because we have not yet prepared our psyches to take control and we have not yet made the positive convictions that permit us to succeed.

When we have negative ideas that supports we can't achieve something, we need to flip it around and consider why we can achieve something. When we have a negative contemplation that something may not work out well, we can alter those contemplations and consider what could work excellently well.

Therefore, when we say that we can't achieve something we need to consider why we can fulfil something. We need to discuss assertions, to assist us to touch base at another positive state of mind. The brain is similar to a garden that needs sustaining. Negative thoughts can obliterate it. We have to uproot the negative ideas furthermore plant new seeds as positive affirmations for the greenery enclosure to develop.

We likewise need to work with lots of systems. The outcomes will show up when we wouldn't dare hope anymore. We need to keep watering the nursery bed of our brain with positive thinking and at exactly that point will things begin to change. So when is this change going to happen?

At the point when are we going to be prepared and when are we going to dispense with the negatives that come into our mindset? Continue doing the activities and the progressions will happen sooner than you anticipate. Trust me when I say this.

So give me a chance to remind you once more, we need to care for the nursery bed of our psyche. We first need to find and after that start uprooting the weeds of our negativity and constraining convictions (weeds). We then need to substitute these weeds with new seeds.

These seeds must be certain and they must be sure considerations that prompt positive sentiments that lead on to positive activities lastly prompt positive results.

Chapter 7

Who Are Your Friends & Associates?

Have you ever heard the truism, you are the company that you keep? In the event that you have, then you comprehend the effective influence that others' demeanours can possibly have on your own ¦ negative or positive. On the other hand, you comprehend that your activities toward others make them act and respond in kind. It can be truly a cycle.

The uplifting news is that it's never past the point where it is possible to change your attitude. You can begin now. Today is the first day of whatever remains of your life. Here are seven stages you can adopt toward adding to a positive mentality today for whatever remains of your life:

Change your vocabulary. The dialect you use impacts the way you think, so take out of your vocabulary words like can't, won't, and disappointment.

Toss the thoughtfulness rebound. Consistently, perform one unselfish demonstration. Keep in mind, your activities "positive or negative " will return to you. Abstain from investing energy with adverse minded individuals and endless grumblers. As the adage goes, Misery loves company.

At whatever point you can, change the subject to a positive one. Be the one individuals see as constantly lively.

Offset every negative bit of news with no less than five positive ones. Stay current with what's happening in the universe, and highlight the great stories in your discussions with others. Turn if I, might I be able to, would I to should, can and will.

Make a list of the attributes, propensities, states of mind and aptitudes that embody the perfect you. At that point, attempt to take after those rules.

When you've read all the stages a couple times, record them and keep them in a spot where you will see them routinely "on the fridge, on your restroom mirror, or around your work area at work. To help you remain focused, think about setting a reminder on your mobile phone to show one of these progressions during the day.

When you put your new project into practice, give careful consideration to the way others respond toward you. You'll see that the constructive words and activities you place out into the world will return to you with the same respect, and you'll see that other constructive minded individuals will incline toward your sunny attitude.

Building up and keeping up a positive mentality demands responsibility and support, after some time.

Chapter 8

Looking Beyond Your Comfort Zone

Having the right outlook about life is very paramount to greater achievements. When you expand your views about the World, you certainly rise to new level of self awareness.

Each of us sustains in our psyche a 'photo of who we are and what we are equipped for accomplishing. We will just endeavour those activities that fall inside of this container of what is conceivable. We dismiss as outlandish anything that falls short. Unmistakably, by growing this container or worldview we can house a greater amount of what we accept is conceivable and as such broaden what we trust we are fit for accomplishing.

A worldview applies an intense impact on the nature of our connections, monetary security, scholarly development, physical wellbeing, an inspirational demeanour or whatever else we beyond a reasonable doubt need. It really controls each aspects of our life.

Our worldview must be alterable - always extending to adjust to changing circumstances and conditions. In the event that we stay bound to a prohibitive worldview, we got to be static. There will be no change to our circumstances, and no development. We get to be casualties of circumstances rather than victors.

Growing the worldview needs creativity and conviction. We have to add to the propensity for considering unheard of options and looking past the self-evident. We are completely allowed to choose where to put our cutoff points. Since we can't know every one of the potential outcomes that lie outside our worldview, our restrictions are all that much, what we choose them to be. Growing the attitude.

I said before that growing our worldview or what we consider conceivable needs genius. Genius needs conviction and an ability to consider choices. We will, notwithstanding, consider options just when we truly trust that alluring results are conceivable. Things being what they are, how would we create conviction?

Nothing advantageous can be accomplished without exertion, so this development procedure is not going to occur incidentally. It will come about because of loyally taking after a couple of fundamental steps:

Build your insight. Libraries, the Internet and experienced individuals are fabulous wellsprings of information. Arm yourself with a specific data.

The higher you study a subject, the more certain you become. Certainty prompts conviction, which prompts belief. Positively, we can't be privy to all things, except our store of learning in particular territories we pick; we trust we can accomplish what we set out to do.

In the event that you consider establishing an Internet business, however just know how to send and get electronic messages, you will have a hard time believing that you can do it. It's inconceivable in light of the fact that it's outside your scope.

Yet, in the event that you study it, comprehend the nuts and bolts about websites and installation frameworks, website improvement and the entire continuum of essentials, then it turns out to be progressively conceivable. Continuously attempt to procure extra data.

Accumulate every one of the certainties you can, representing whatever it is you trust you can do. Certainties give a guide and help keep you destined for success. Apply insight. Astuteness is fundamentally an ability to think, fortified by applying a scholarly procedure to evaluate the certainties. These actualities are deliberately adjusted with feelings. There's an enthusiastic component in all that we think and do, yet depending exclusively on feelings to settle on a choice can prompt extremely unwelcome results. Keep in mind; never cut down a dead tree during the winter.

Conceptualize your thoughts and ideas. Try not to dismiss any thought at first, paying little respect to how unreasonable, crazy or silly it shows up. In numerous examples, a thought of extraordinary quality has come about because of this kind of mental activity. It is likewise an incredible course to alternative or lateral mentality.

At long last, make a move. The most phenomenal thoughts and arrangements are of no quantifiable worth until they are acted upon. Acting on them is presumably the hardest stage. Consider what number of awesome thoughts you have had that blurred into obscurity in light of the fact that you ceased just before the 'make a move' part.

The obstructions to making a move

Any sort of result, whether business oriented or individual, is just impractical without activity. The best-laid arrangements are useless until they are followed up on. In any case, while there evidently are obstacles to making a move, they are not unbeatable.

Here are some of the obstacles to making a move, and suggestions on how these may be surmounted.

1. Absence of self-confidence or self-esteem

Not being persuaded that we possess what is needed to make something conceivable. Painstakingly recognize what it is you need to possess that you don't currently own, and then list out specific targets that will lead you to gain them.

Make little strides and make the targets achievable. Achievement nourishes on itself. As you perform every target, it urges you to proceed onward to more driven ones.

2. Absence of direction, confusion or plain laziness

Review your objectives once more. Make them clear and follow the S.A.D. dictum - specific, achievable and desirable. They must be specific or you will get sidetracked. They must be achievable or you will get demoralized, and they should unquestionably be desirable, or you will lose purpose halfway.

3. Absence of information, conviction, or belief

This has already been explained. See above.

4. Resistance to change

People avert change, and lean toward the known than the untried on the grounds that it gives them a misguided feeling that all is well and good. They stick to the norms, and in the end getting to be tolerating of circumstances that are unsavoury or that have stopped to be helpful or profitable.

What number of married women stay in the marriage on the grounds that they are reluctant to leave naturally despite being abused? Being free lies outside their scope, and is in this manner impractical.

5. No optional thinking

Search for choices. Extend your views about the world. Very often, we hook onto one thought, and neglect to practice the freedom of optional consideration. On the off chance that we do not have the requirements to make an interpretation of this one thought enthusiastically, we relinquish the entire thing. Yet, there is often times when an optional alternative would function pretty much too, or even better.

6. Falling for a wait-and-see mode

This is generally the consequence of trepidation, brought on by not taking the suggestions given above. We choose to hold up till everything is impeccable, and conditions are simply right. Yet, conditions don't right themselves. You right them. Sitting tight for wonderfully right conditions is similar to holding up to strike a lottery. They are both long shots.

Keep in mind, conditions can never be flawless, and they don't need to be. Make them flawless them as you come. Upgrades come most times in small packages.

You can't control activities that are reliant on

others. Sitting tight for another person to make the ideal conditions for you is as a rule unreasonably hopeful.

It is difficult to envision each probability, inevitability or result. You manage them as they emerge. Immaculate conditions sometimes arrive without so much effort.

7. Past disappointments

Remember that nobody has accomplished anything of quality without a progression of disappointments. Painstakingly break down why you fizzled. Is it in light of something you ought to have done, yet didn't? Maybe it was something you shouldn't have done, however you did.

What were the circumstances then that added to the disappointment? Have they changed? If not, would you be able to alter them now to expand your shots of accomplishment?

Make a move. Inquire of yourself, 'What's the drawback? What do I lose by making a move instead of doing nothing?"

"When I have chosen that something should be done, - I act." Now that is a triumphant mental state of mind.

Chapter 9

Be Aware of the Key 12 Universal Laws

"Have you ever tried to drive to a destination that you have never visited before and never knew anything about? Can you remember how many times you missed your way, the turnings and had to start all over again? Did you think a map or satellite navigator would have been very useful to you at that point in time?

That's what it feels like when we try to navigate through life without understanding that there are various laws of Nature (Universal laws) to abide by in order to win the game of life.

When we choose to ignore the natural Laws of the Universe, we do not need to be reminded that very often, we will experience struggle, resistance, unfulfilled destiny, pain, lack of direction etc .

It has always been in the nature of humanity to believe mostly in the things we can see, feel, taste, hear or touch while doubting anything else that is beyond the perception of our immediate senses. However, whether you believe it or not, these Universal Laws influence our everyday lives and you cannot change that.

You can liken these Universal Laws to a very deep root of a tree buried underground which the ordinary eyes cannot see and yet, the root exerts so much influence on the tree because without the root, a tree cannot stand.

Here is a brief outline of the key 12 Universal Laws:

1. The Law of Divine Oneness

The Law of Divine Oneness is the first of the 12 Universal Laws and it helps us to understand that in this World we live, everything is connected to everything else. Every thought, words, actions and beliefs of ours affect others and the universe around us irrespective of whether the people are near or far away, in other words, beyond time and space.

2. The Law of Vibration

The Law of Vibration states that everything in the Universe vibrates, moves, and travels in circular patterns. The same principle of vibration in the physical world apply to our feelings, desires, thoughts, dreams and will. Each sound, thought or thing has its own unique vibrational frequency. When you hear people say 'like attracts like', they are actually referring to how a vibrational energy can resonate with or is attracted to the same or a similar vibrational energy.

Basically, this is the reason why what others do or

say affect us directly or indirectly. However, if you are not happy with your current vibration, you will need to make a conscious choice to focus your energy more on positive emotions and less on negative emotions in order to raise your vibration higher beyond the one you do not want in your life.

If you do not want more bad news coming to you, do not be the one to start spreading it around to others. By giving others that which you desire, you indirectly increase that which comes back to you.

3. The Law of Action

The Law of Action must be applied in order for us to manifest things on earth. Therefore, we must engage in actions that support our words, feelings, vision, thoughts, dreams and emotions. These actions will bring us manifestation of various results which are dependent on our specifically chosen words, thoughts, dreams, and emotions.

4. The Law of Correspondence

The Law of Correspondence basically puts us in the drivers' seat of our own lives. Our outer world is a direct reflection of our inner world, therefore, we need to accept responsibility for our own lives.

Another good example for this law is the fact that in the physical world, energy, vibration, light and motion have their corresponding principles in the Universe. This explains the relationship between the world of the 'infinite small' and the 'infinite large' otherwise called Microcosm and Macrocosm respectively.

5. The Law of Cause and Effect

The Law of Cause and Effect states that nothing

happens by chance or outside the Universal Laws. This means that, we have to take responsibility for everything that happens in our lives. Every action has an equal reaction or consequence and it is what we sow that we reap. You cannot plant a hibiscus flower and expect to reap a Rose flower. In other words, every thought, action, words are full of energy and whatever we send out returns to us.

6. The Law of Compensation

This Law of Compensation is the extended arm of the Law of Cause and Effect which is applied to abundance and blessings that flow into our lives in the form of friendships, gifts, money, inheritances and other forms of blessings. These various forms of compensation are the visible effects of our direct and indirect actions carried out throughout our lives.

7. The Law of Attraction

This Law of Attraction shows how we create the events, people and things that come into our lives. All our thoughts, words, feelings and actions give out energies which, likewise attract like energies.

Positive energies will always attract positive energies while negative energies will always attract negative energies. It doesn't matter whether you want the negative or not. What you place your attention on, is what you attract into your life.

On the other hand, if you do not like the negative, you just need to raise your vibration higher and away from it in order to fully apply this Law of Attraction to work for you. For example, when anyone starts out thinking negatively, their vibration is lowered. As the focus on the problem rather than the solution becomes intense, the size and number of the problem will magnify as that's where the person's focus is.

8. The Law of Perpetual Transmutation of Energy

The Law of Perpetual Transmutation of Energy is a powerful one. It states that we all have power within us to change any condition in our lives that we are not happy with. Higher energy vibration will definitely consume and transform lower ones. Therefore, we can change the energies in our lives by understanding the Universal Laws and applying the principles in such a way as to effect a positive change in our lives.

9. The Law of Relativity

The Law of Relativity states that each person will receive series of situations or problems for the purpose of strengthening the 'inner light' within us. This law makes it possible for us to stay connected to our hearts when we proceed to solve the problems or remedy the situation which is a 'test' for us.

This law also teaches us to compare our situations to other people's problems and put everything into its right perspective. No matter how bad we perceive our situations to be, there is always someone who is in a more difficult or worst situation thereby making it all relative. Nobody is ever given a problem they will be unable to handle as we already have the ability to handle them. Do not spend your time looking for happiness from the outside as it already lies within you.

10. The Law of Polarity

The Law of Polarity states that everything is on a continuum and has an opposite. There has to be darkness so that we might appreciate Light. There is Solid and liquid and we can see and feel the difference. We have the ability to suppress and transform undesirable thoughts by focusing on the opposite thought thereby bringing the desired positive change. This could also be likened to the law of mental vibration.

11. The Law of Rhythm

The Law of Rhythm states that everything vibrates and moves to a certain rhythm. This rhythm establishes cycles, seasons, patterns, and stages of development. Each cycle is a reflection of the regularity of God's universe. To master each rhythm, you must rise above any negative part of the cycle.

12. The Law of Gender

The Law of Gender states that everything has its masculine (yang) and feminine (yin) principles, and that these are the basis for all creation in the Universe. As spiritual beings, we must ensure that there is a balance between the masculine and feminine energies within us in order for us to become true co-creators with God." - *(reproduced with permission from the original author; Genevieve Flight)*

Chapter 10

Give Out What
You Want Back

How to attract what you need

By what method would you be able to get the things you need in life? In what manner would you be able to get the adoration, wellbeing, cash and joy you crave? Numerous individuals trust diligent work will get the things they cherish. For most, that appears to work. Be that as it may, a few individuals work sun up to twilight and still don't have the life they crave.

A few individuals appear to have the Midas touch. They appear to draw in riches. They may even incidentally lose their riches - recall Donald Trump's business liquidation? Presently Trump's name is synonymous with wealth. The mystery may be the Law of Attraction. The Law of Attraction states: What you consider you realize.

From the earliest starting point he appeared to be

giving up that nothing would work out. What's more, it didn't. He was the sort of man who made a big deal about himself - he worked his way up to an administration work. One day, he came back from a business trip just to come back to a pink slip - he'd been let go. What did he do? He took his severance and began his own organization. It didn't work out.

He was out of cash and he moved back in with his elderly folks. This was after he raised 2 offspring he could call his own. At the time he said, "In some cases I have a tendency to be demoralized, however I can't concentrate on that." And he didn't. He appeared to KNOW he merited better and was fit for better. What was the deal? He accepted a vocation as a representative in a store, and then discovered another position.

Presently he's extremely fruitful, remarried, has 3 more delightful youngsters and lives in major houses. From the earliest starting point he was persuaded that he was a winner, regardless of what life tossed at him. Comparative circumstances, diverse results. A few individuals trust regardless of what they do, nothing will pan out.

Other individuals trust that achievement is in store for them. Who's privileged? They both are. The Law of Attraction expresses that whatever you give your centre to shows itself in your life. The vast majority concentrate on current circumstances, so their lives keep on showing comparative circumstances.

The key is to concentrate on what you need and would like to see happen in your life. To show that it is what you need, concentrate your attention on that specific need. This is the key; imagine how it feels to have exactly what you need.

If you are interested in finding an adorable new

relationship, just imagine and feel yourself encountering a cherishing relationship. If you would like to improve your general wellbeing, imagine how you'd feel living in wellness. If your interest is that you need to be rich, imagine how you'd feel with bounteous wealth.

State what you need just as you have it NOW. For illustrations: I now appreciate hearty wellbeing and feel solid. It feels awesome. I am now pleased driving my shiny, new, red vehicle. I now look affectionately into the eyes of a kind, clever man and feel his adoration for me.

Over 100 years ago, James Allen said in 'As a Man Thinketh' "The spirit draws in that which it subtly harbours; what it adores, furthermore that which it fears." Deliberately choose what you need to centre your consideration on. Concentrate and visualise achieving most of your intended result and watch it happen.

Chapter 11

Opportunities are Changes

How to be successful at anything

Setting objectives and dreams is something that numerous individuals have prepared on, yet still many individuals will never accomplish their objectives. Why would that be? The response to this is exceptionally basic, yet it can likewise be extremely difficult to comprehend. Since the answer is, essentially, that YOU are the distinction and not what you have or who you are, but how you approach your objectives matter.

Everyone encounters some sort of contention around the things they need. It may be that you need to purchase new garments, however you know the cash ought to go on your credit. Then again you may need to spend the weekend at home, because you know your family hasn't seen you in a while. These sorts of contentions we manage constantly, likely without notwithstanding contemplating it excessively.

In any case, imagine a scenario where one of your huge objectives is to be closer with your family, and you have a contention that you need to stay at home that weekend. You need to choose which is more vital.

So what's this got in common with the business world? Well - a great many people begin their own particular business in light of the fact that they have seen another person having achievement here, and it is something that they feel they could do.

In the web world, that frequently means joining an arrangement or some likeness thereof, as a rule with a guide. So what has the effect between the individual who joins that framework and changes their life and the individual who does not? The framework is the same, the capacities are the same, even the measure of cash and time to contribute are the same, yet one individual turns into a tycoon while alternate announces that same opportunity till now as another trick.

The contrast between these two individuals is the manner by which they handle clashes. Being completely focused around the accomplishment of your business is the key first step - with totally everything else taking a rearward sitting arrangement.

In the matter of Saturday night when you would regularly invest energy with your family - what happens to your business? On the off chance that you are half dead from a taxing day at work - what happens to your publicizing arrangement for that night? On the off chance that you need to settle on the choice between placing cash into publicizing or purchasing new garments - will your garments last one more month?

Disappointment does not happen as a solitary, enormous occasion - it happens as a consequence of some little, terrible choices every day. In the same way, achievement is not joined by a loud fanfare and firecrackers - it shows up as you use sound judgment every day. In the event that you choose to put on weight - you would do nothing more than choose to eat pizza and chocolate rather than eating mixed fresh fruits, green vegetables and all kinds of legumes.

Also, settling on the right choices for your business at every stride is all that you require for achievement. That is in some cases simpler said than done, however here's the way I have come to approach this:

Firstly, pick your main 3 objectives. One is far superior, however the greater part of us have a not insignificant record to browse - perhaps your business, another vehicle and a better house, for instance. Be that as it may, you need to have a little focus to concentrate on - so don't pick objectives that will instantly clash with one another, for instance establishing another business and playing golf consistently, for instance.

Next, get clear on those objectives - use ALL your imagination procedures and truly get into that place. This is an activity that you will need to do every day as you begin this procedure; however the primary concern is that you get into the skin of the individual that you will get to be whenever you accomplish those objectives.

At last, begin being that individual every single day. So every time you need to settle on a choice, whether it's a noteworthy one or simply choosing to go to lunch, you are settling on that choice as your new persona. The greater amount of your choices that originate from that place, the quicker you will get to your objective - then your life will turn out to be precisely as you envisioned it! It's sheltered to say that this methodology will include sacrifices.

Be that as it may, you have a decision here - you can live with the torment of control and centre for a brief while so as to have the life you had always wanted, or you can live with the agony of disappointment and "imagine a scenario where" for whatever remains of your life.

Learn this aptitude and you can be carrying on with the sort of life most don't even endeavour to hope for - continue floating from choice to choice and you will never see your maximum capacity.

Chapter 12

Creating Self-Awareness & Self-discipline

How to develop self confidence

When you have high fearlessness you will see that your life enhances radically, however numerous individuals experience the ill effects of low self-esteem around the globe. It is vital for everybody to be made mindful of how to have self-assurance that is never going to falter.

It is not as troublesome as it appears to enhance your self-discipline. You simply need to figure out the best approach to have the high self awareness you need to be glad in life and that is by just transforming the way you reason.

You may not understand it, but rather the way you think impacts all that you do in your life each and every day. There is no real way to do anything in your existence without your considerations meddling.

That is the reason you have to take control of the way you see yourself so as to enhance the way you feel and take a good look at yourself. The individuals that have the high confidence are the ones that contemplate themselves and everything that happens throughout their life.

You have known that having positive intuition coupled with the need to be fearless stands out among the best approaches to use and enhance how you feel about yourself. That's the reason why you have to master approaches to use to help you begin thinking emphatically. There are various exercises that you can do that will help you build a positive mindset and improve self confidence.

A couple of activities that could possibly be done by anybody include:

1. Say positive affirmations once, twice or three times daily

2. Gather round yourself steady and constructive individuals

3. Use self development books, eBooks, Youtube videos, articles, CDs, DVDs and whatever else is positive and helpful. Search online and you will find many of them.

4. Put yourself first and deal with yourself so you like yourself.

5. Trust yourself and acknowledge you are a human that is going to commit errors.

Learn from them and see them as a chance to develop and move forward.

These are only a couple of the ways that you can choose to use every one of them to help you enhance the way you see yourself. Anybody that can roll out this improvement will truly enhance their lifestyle and that is dependably a decent objective to pursue for everybody.

After you discover how to change the way you think consistently to a positive one, you will have made sense of the most intense route for truly enhancing your fearlessness. Since you have the data required about how to have self-assurance, you have to start utilizing it immediately to help you enhance your self-assurance and your life.

How to build Self Belief

Genuine confidence is an uncommon blessing that we ascribe to ourselves. Therapists say that the best way to accomplish it is to act naturally. Pretending and claiming to be somebody else, to pick up acknowledgment or social acknowledgment, disintegrates your certainty in light of the fact that you are always perplexed that others will find your falsification and misdirection.

Incredible Beginnings - Early Impressions

In adolescence, you begin with a lot of certainty and confidence. In any case, if the individuals throughout your life and environs are not steady, but rather are judgmental and discriminating, you rapidly start to question your worth, lose self-conviction, and start to look for support by attempting to change the parts of your conduct that are focused by the cynicism of other people.

Being receptive and helpless in youth, your

trepidation of dismissal sets in and you look for regard through pretending; endeavouring to persuade others that you think, feel and go about as they do, with a specific end goal to fit in and be acknowledged.

Where did YOU Go?

Always controlling your genuine emotions and practices and curbing them, in the long run prompts a development of anxiety, misery and outrage. These feelings can influence your wellbeing and bliss; which is the reason it is basic to your prosperity that you re-associate with yourself, and settle on a cognizant choice to be consistent with your own particular emotions, wishes, intrigues and needs.

Asking Tough Self discovery Questions

The most ideal approach to recover and revamp certainty is to find once more the genuine you and locate your self-conviction. To do this you need to wind up mindful of your great qualities and characteristics. Keeping a diary of what you like about yourself is an incredible first step. Being reflective and truly analysing your own one of a kind quality is difficult. Incorporate the perceptions of individuals you think about and trust, in your diary.

What do your loved ones respect about you and give you acclaim and support about? Do you get the greater part of your own acceptance from outside sources? How frequently do those outer sources truly convey fulfilment and enduring satisfaction to your life? Infrequently, is the way a large portion of us would answer that question. It's now or never to begin discovering genuine motivations to adore yourself as you really seem to be, right now in your life.

Building Confidence

Commend your qualities and acknowledge your shortcomings on the grounds that everybody has both positive and negative properties. Try not to harp on what you see are your disappointments. Keeping positive is fundamental. Keep in mind that each individual is considerably more than simply the total of their victories and disappointments. Life and the people in it are unpredictable and extraordinary. Depicting anybody as either great or terrible is only an over-disentanglement of the human condition.

Every individual has worth and conveys a wide range of extremely valuable qualities to this world. You may be an extremely innovative, interesting, enchanting and dependable individual. Maybe you are very educated and have a need to support others, and have any kind of effect on the planet. When you concentrate on who you are, and what you do that is well done and profitable, and also, what you genuinely appreciate; you start to be subjective, and locate your own particular legitimate self.

Staying Focused

When you centre your consideration on the advantageous and positive properties that you have, without apologizing for what you see are your failings and deficiencies; your self-uncertainty will start to lessen. Concentrate on loving "you" and surround yourself with empowering connections, as frequently as would be prudent.

Always make out time to assess and re-evaluate your commitments in order to be sure you are on the right track towards achieving what you want in life.

Recaptured Confidence

Certainty comes into your life when you hold yourself in high respect and task a practical and positive picture that you really have confidence in. Getting settled with the genuine you, will be liberating, and will discharge the outrage and disappointment you felt when you attempted to shroud your real self. There is a lot of joy in life, and when you are consistent with yourself, satisfaction and happiness will be next.

5 simple steps for building self confidence

Almost all tasks or objectives of any size or significance need a few stages over a stretch of time for it to be finished. Anything even a little bit muddled needs arrangement, know-how and determination through a few stages over a span of time. All that is additionally valid about anything like deciding to gain more self regard. Here's the means by which you can do only that in 5 straightforward steps.

Step 1. Quit the critic within you

This is truly vital since you have to begin saying positive things in regards to yourself as an imperative stride in growing more self esteem. Start your day before your mirror and let yourself know how significant you are... On the off chance that you don't generally do this, then you are feeling the loss of an essential and successful approach to grow more self regard.

Step 2. Participate in some physical activity

This can be a truly basic step that will require your full consideration and focus. You must do it along these lines: Exercise helps a great deal on creating more grounded self regard. The key motivation behind why you'll require this is physical activity makes you feel more appealing and agreeable around other individuals.

Step 3. Transform your state of mind

What we are doing here is to create a new way of thinking. As we start to break the programmed thinking cycle, we can turn out to be more mindful of a scope of sentiments that may be happening in light of our self-talk. Likewise, it's to realize that understanding conduct can be the window to change. When we distinguish the connection between our thoughts and emotions and our triggers, we stand a chance in changing our conduct.

Step 4. Don`t blame yourself for past issues

To clarify and expand on that a bit, the past is behind you and you cannot transform it but rather you have a fresh brand new day today. Go ahead and use it to do something positive...

Step 5. Start offering more to the individuals around you

Additionally, when you do things for another person, you are making a constructive commitment and you start to feel more important, which thus lifts your spirits and raises your own self-esteem.

At the end, when you have implemented the aforementioned tips totally, you will have succeeded and after this can settle-back and relish the advantages of this achievement. Pat yourself on the back, be a bit satisfied with yourself because you set out to work on your life goals and you essentially succeeded! Now appreciate it!

On the off chance that you did obey the above tips, you will be in a better position to improve and have the good luck in many things you concentrate on.

Tips on developing self discipline

Many individuals frequently feel control is the unlucky deficiency of flexibility. In any case, it is really the precise opposite. Self-control will help you accomplish genuine flexibility. Why? Since, undisciplined people are for the most part like slaves to wild hungers, states of mind and interests. Likewise, a certain level of order is additionally needed for figuring out how to be outstandingly great in different fields, might it be music, games, or any kind of task.

So the question is; what is the best way to achieve self-control?. Developing self-control is doubtlessly not an overnight process. It can regularly need making yields and renouncing certain rushes and joys. On the off chance that you discover yourself battling with control, the uplifting news is, it can be developed. Here are a few tips to bail you out:

Self- Discipline

Self discipline directs your choices and conduct on what you believe is best, paying little mind to how you feel and what you need in that particular minute. It is consequently vital to set aside time to know yourself with a specific end goal to create discipline.

Your choices, needs and conduct basically mirror

your qualities and objectives. The procedure of self information needs you to invest energy for investigation and thoughtfulness. Frequently, the most ideal approach to do this is to record your desire, objectives and dreams. You can expound on yourself, what you cherish most and how you see yourself as an individual.

Conscious Awareness

Accomplishing and authorizing self-control additionally depends on your cognizant familiarity with what you are doing and what you are not doing. Absence of familiarity with conduct is a quality of somebody undisciplined.

As you attempt to build your self-control, you become more mindful of your activities and catch yourself doing things that reek of indiscipline, for example, skipping activity, revelling on consumables that are terrible for your wellbeing or investing an excess of energy surfing the web.

As said, it will need time and duty to create self-control. The key here is to figure out how to be mindful and distinguish activities that should be remedied. This will give you the chance to rectify and adjust your choices and activities as per your qualities and objectives.

Your responsibility to Self-discipline

It is insufficient that you distinguish your qualities and objectives. An inner duty is needed to adhere to a firm resolve and have the capacity to make the penances you have to make. Responsibility is needed in settling on little regular choices, for example, whether to disregard your alert and fall back to rest, hit the snooze key or get up and do what you have to do.

Bravery

Developing self-control is hard. It needs you to conflict with interests, longings and mind-sets. You have to have the fearlessness to make the hard and likewise excruciating choices. As you begin, you will begin gathering little triumphs against allurements and impediments. After some time, through the valour to be predictable, you will have the capacity to develop and add to your self-control, and making hard choices and important penances will fall into place easily.

Inside Coaching

As you face challenges along the way, you should always help yourself to remember your objectives, summon up resolve and boldness to put forth a valiant effort and strengthen your dedication. By having the capacity to develop self-restraint, you will have the capacity to increase full control of your life and change the course of your wellbeing, vocation, individual relations and other essential parts of life.

Chapter 13

What Are Your Passions?

Identify your Passions

I unequivocally trust that everybody can follow their dreams - everything we require involves making an arrangement. However, how do you begin detailing that arrangement in the event that you don't have a smart idea of what precisely your obsession is? Take after these steps and you will have the first step - recognizing your actual purpose and the chances you could seek after that will take advantage of the delight and motivation behind carrying on with the life you generally craved to live.

1. Indulge in the fun and euphoria

Look at what in your life presents to you a feeling of delight. What does fun mean to you? Compose a list of things and put a start next to the first three. Consider your youth. What did you want to do then? What diversions and past-times do you have? What did you use to do before life turned out to be excessively time consuming? What gives you that sentiment of prosperity? What puts a smile on your face? What could possibly make you laugh?

2. Which of these activities are significant to you?

Baking a cake is a good fun for quite a lot of people and yet genuinely significant to just a few. Significance is an exceptionally individual thing and very often this resonates with a part of you. What exercises present to you a profound level of fulfilment?

What connections exist between the exercises that are more noteworthy to you? Attempt to restrict it down and get as particular as could be expected under the circumstances.

In the event that you trust that it is a piece of your motivation to help individuals, and then tighten it down to how you might most want to help individuals. Consider both the ways you appreciate helping and those you don't.

Case in point for me nursing would be high on my priorities of things I would prefer not to do. Additionally, as a case, I want to help individuals with positive things instead of helping them through negative things.

3. What are your present skills and gifts?

Display them all, everything from having the capacity to put on a duvet spread in less than 5 minutes to having the capacity to make yourself understood by somebody who does not speak the same dialect as you do. Attempt to truly realize totally new possibilities.

Ask individuals who know you well to help as now and then an expertise feels so normal to us we accept everybody has it. It is safe to say that you are better than average at making individuals feel great around you? Have you sorted out your office with the goal that everything is close by? Additionally write down areas in which you appreciate learning and could undoubtedly gain new skills and abilities in.

4. What are your current situations?

Do you require a specific wage level? Do you have any wellbeing difficulties? Do you have obligations throughout your life that would need to be mulled over, for example, caring for youngsters or an elderly relative? Do you have a partner who moves consistently because of the military or work related reasons? Consider everything that shapes your life that should be thought seriously about.

5. Take the list you wrote initially & begin conceptualizing possible opportunities

Go W-I-D-E here. On the off chance that singing is high up on your list don't simply zoom in on rock star, consider everything from singing jingles to karaoke! Let the thoughts permeate in your mind for a couple of days and each time you think about another prospect record it - regardless of the fact that it's something you wouldn't really take up as you never can tell what can be gained from one thought.

For instance you may know you would never feel the urge to own an eatery yet, perhaps you would love to be an eatery detractor or have a site given to nearby eateries.

Take a look at your 5 different records and begin searching for shared traits and things which fit in all cases. Search for means that you could begin edging towards living your dreams. What might be your next step? Research? Mastering another occupation? Setting cash aside so you can in the long run quit your occupation?

What might be the following steps after that? By putting down the next few stages, you have built yourself an arrangement that will keep on growing until you have made the life that you generally longed for and you will have achieved it slowly and carefully.

How to find your dream job

We have all been born with one special endowment and gift, yet a large number of us have not been eager to discover them, investigate, create or express those qualities. Hence a large number of us have ended up in occupations which don't permit us to express who we truly are.

The primary efforts to begin to discover your fantasy work, includes distinguishing your exceptional qualities, blessings and gifts, what you are energetic about and where you can have any kind of effect.

In case you're drained constantly, you would prefer not to get up in the morning, you are not keen on what you are doing, you can't focus at work any longer, and you may need to consider changing your occupation or profession.

Begin by noting the following "self-assessment" questions to incite thinking and to start your voyage towards reason, satisfaction and significance.

Locate a peaceful spot where you won't be exasperated. Unwind your body and brain. Set aside as much time as you have to record your answers. Discharge all points of confinement and permit yourself to dream about the vocation you were destined to do.

1. What task would you want to do on the off chance that you had all the cash, time and assets you required as of now, or if all occupations paid identical salaries?

2. What motivates you? What do you appreciate most regarding existence?

3. What are your qualities? Which values would you like to showcase via your work?

4. What comes regularly and simply to you? What do you achieve without stress?

5. What are your qualities, abilities and endowments? What are your normal capacities?

    Record them and invest some energy thinking about your replies. At that point ask your loved ones to answer this question for you. What is their impression of your aptitudes and capacities? What do they believe you are great at? Ask them what they see is a blessing that you give to the world. Now and then others can help us see what we are blind to.

6. What is absent from your job now? What was absent from your past occupations? Was there anything you needed to do, yet have abstained for reasons unknown?

Set aside as much time as you have to assess yourself utilizing these inquiries until you are fulfilled by your answers which will give you some comprehensive details about your vocation course. Confucius said, "Discover an occupation you appreciate, and you'll never work a day in your life.

Chapter 14

What Influences
Your Mind?

How To Unlock The Power Of Your Mind

The power of the human mind (personality) is something that excites the entire world till today. Such a great amount has been discovered concerning it yet despite everything we need to know to such an extent.

Actually the idea of wasting the power of mind should not to be supported at all. It is really significant and in actuality we can use this huge force source to enhance our lives in a major way. We can put this to great use and accomplish whatever we need or yearn for in life.

The world was affected by the idea of the authority of the psyche after the book named The Secret and the motion picture named the same was debuted to the business sector. The individuals got to be mindful of the Laws of Attraction and its utility in our lives.

The Laws of Attraction demonstrated that the contemplations of an individual are vital since the considerations just draw in the things that we seek for and those which will improve our lives in the nearest future.

The principle point is that your brain will show whatever you reason. What a great many people don't understand is that this happens whether you effectively get it going or not. So begin to use the authority of the mind to deliberately build the life you need.

As it were, you can see this impact of mind authority at work in clinical trials where it is known as the placebo impact. It's about mind over matter. When you consider something; rather, when you have faith in something, the force of the brain can get it going.

Without a doubt you have seen individuals "think" themselves ill, and you have seen them "think" themselves well. Our psyche authority is fantastic.

There may be another case of this hypothesis. We may find that at some point when we get up from rest in the morning and imagine that this day will be an ordinary day or a not very great day, it truly ends up being one or the other.

Also, it truly isn't simply incidental. Everything happens for a reason and the reason is your mind's authority.

Sadly, you may have an issue with the exploratory proof, yet there is enough. Quantum mechanics clarifies that there isn't matter on a subatomic level and it's quite plainly energy. While this is valid, there are investigations continually being done that makes us understand that vitality exists on account of the onlooker. It genuinely is the major force behind the brain.

All so called 'paranormal' powers such as telepathy and other psychic or intuitive powers can be explained using Quantum physics. There is nothing "extraordinary" about them except that you have to devote your time learning how to acquire these gifts. Despite the fact that a large number of us consider this to be phony Television, it's quite of the Quantum Physics Theory. Therefore, nothing is solid, but rather they are energy which our minds have the power to create and utilise.

You've likely officially encountered this a period or two without acknowledging it. Perhaps you were carving coupons and that inward voice lets you know that if you don't stop you'll wind up cutting your hand. At that point obviously you didn't listen to this hogwash and all of a sudden you stick your other hand with the scissors. Without a doubt, it might not have happened precisely like this, but rather you get the drift. Let's contemplate on the stages expected to guide your psyche energy to making what you need.

At first, there must be an objective set in our mind and it must be done in a careful manner. The objective however ought not to contain anything that is not clear. On the off chance that it is a measure of cash that we have set in our brain, the sum must be unmistakably carved in our contemplations. After this we must commute every one of our considerations and psyche exercises to this objective and will soon see the outcome.

Exempt yourself far from disturbing pressures. Keep that exertion consistent. Attempt to clear your psyche of the typical example of thirty unique considerations running without a moment's delay.

There are some people who have mastered how to direct and tackle their brain energy to incredible degrees.

They remain totally centred around the objective they need to accomplish in life and subsequently have the capacity to shape their life in a superior manner.

They concentrate on particular targets and put the greater part of their endeavours towards achieving their goal, utilizing the full force of their minds. This is the thing that gets it going; it's tougher than it sounds on paper, however it's something that every one of us can accomplish in the event that we put our concentrations to it.

Envision totally changing your life by effectively tuning in the impact your psyche has on your world. Say that you needed another house. You need that new house so much that it very nearly turns into a fixation. You fantasize it constantly; you have even arranged the scene and the colour of the main washroom.

Consistently, you begin with a list of undertakings that will pull you closer to dreams of owning a house of your own. You arrange it; you consider colour plans and finishing. Inevitably, this will support your execution at work; it will urge you to spare, or to curtail your debt.

What will be your feeling if suddenly your fantasy home became available on the market and you had the capacity to bear the cost of it? Really great right! Imagine a scenario in which in twelve months you really own it. These are the sorts of things you can do to make your life comprehensively better. On the off chance that there is anything we suggest as your next objective, it must be to take a vacation. Everybody needs them, particularly in the event that you never take one.

More or less our psyche is truly a powerhouse that has no bound to the outlandish things it can do. We ought to not therefore have any questions to the abilities of the human personality.

Preparing your Mind can turn your life around

The human cognizance is the consciousness of oneself as a being that thinks and learns. Consider the distinction between your cognizance and its nearest connection, enthusiastic mindfulness. We as a general public have gotten to be talented translators of how dreams, apprehensions, clashes and passionate connection influences our encounters and activities.

Notwithstanding our abnormal state of enthusiastic mindfulness, few of us accomplish an abnormal state of brain awareness. Generally instructed and modern individuals have for all intents and purposes no familiarity with how they take care of issues, find thoughts, acclimatize and oversee data, or adjust to change.

Is it essential to build up your mental ability? A human personality is an instrument of colossal force. The similitude between the workings of your psyche and the brain of a noteworthy researcher, (for example, Einstein) or a progressive mastermind, for example, Freud are extraordinary, while the distinctions are unpretentious.

To maximize the use of your brain, you should be mindful of what it does as you think and learn. Weird as it may appear, you just need to figure out how to use the capacity of the brain that you as of now have. That is the reason mind awareness is such a capable resource. With the right methods, you can prepare your psyche and enhance your memory and quicken your learning.

You can never absolutely be in control of your brain any more than you could ever thoroughly be in control of your body, however, you can control it. Your heart continues thumping, your lungs continue breathing, your ears continue hearing, and whatever is left of our body continues working, generally, whether you instruct it to or not. In the same way, your psyche continues absorbing data and reinterpreting your experience. Be that as it may, nor are you obliged to let your brain control you.

Think as far as the relationship with your body. You can advise your eyes where to look and your feet where to step. With activity you can impact how far you can run, and with preparation you can even influence how quickly your heart thumps.

By educating your memory, in the event that you study your brain and comprehend it, it will surpass your desires. On the off chance that you constantly prepare your psyche with the right memory methods, it will serve you well in years to come.

With unpretentious changes as you would notice in your observation abilities, you can direct your own particular learning in the same sort of way that an administration controls a nation's economy. Financial experts offer strategies for the administration to stay away from both an over warmed inflationary economy and monetary wretchedness. They track business cycles and recommend solutions to manage the excesses that could crash economic development anytime.

Your brain experiences learning cycles in identical way that the economy experiences business cycles. On the off chance that you comprehend the repetitive examples you could call your own brain, you will have the capacity to keep the development you could call your own psyche enchantment on trick too.

Could brain preparation help you in this present reality? Most likely! A few individuals have contended for a considerable length of time that you will improve at mastering even a game, for example, tennis in the event that you get to be aware of how your brain normally learns. The same rule applies to most areas of encounters.

Adjusting to life in the data age will basically be the same as adjusting to whatever other sensational changes in living situations. That can mean just a sole purpose, later on, considerably more than some time recently, you will need to depend on your special capabilities alone. That ought not to be any reason for alert. Your regular capacity is completely sufficient so long as you are capable of putting it to great use.

Accomplishment in life is dictated by the decisions we take. The decisions we make are controlled by how we think and use our mental ability. Through the span of your lifetime, examples of feeling that impact all your choice making are produced. In this way, most would agree the main way you can influence a result in your life is to roll out improvements to your thinking mentality.

So you can roll out the fundamental improvements to your life, it is useful to get a simple comprehension of how the mind functions. The brain has been portrayed as - the seat of reasoning'. The mind is a confounded organ that partitions up distinctive assignments among its different parts.

You may not be mindful that we sort of have two brains - left and right. This is on account that our mind is isolated into two different parts that perform distinctive obligations.

The left half of your brain is best at preparing small details, concocting speculations, working with rationale to take care of issues and working our arrangements. It is the left hand side of the brain that is used the most at school. In this manner, measuring its adequacy is much less demanding.

The right hand part of the brain is excellent at imagining the comprehensive view, concocting innovative thoughts regarding the future and asking the big questions. The right hand side uses instinct rather than rationale in its thinking.

Individuals with an inclination for utilizing the right side tend to battle more with established school learning. Ordinarily, they flourish in unstructured learning situations that let them investigate the world.

To be genuinely effective, you need both sides of your brain to be functioning in amicability with each other. A coherent very much requested personality that is fit for snippets of instinctive splendour is an imposing instrument.

For a moment, consider the part of the brain you depend on the most in view of what you now think about it. Does your utilization incline towards 50% of the brain or do you use both sides?

The mystery of getting an adjusted personality is to practice it consistently. Our psyches are getting it done when they are being invigorated. Approach your mind with deference and the future prizes could be huge.

We keep our bodies exercising so as to look youthful, solid and fit, and the cerebrum is the same. A few researchers trust that individuals who do cerebrum exercises are more averse to getting Alzheimer's disease.

Researchers have recommended that the mind's unstable memory can improve with preparing undertakings, for example, remembering the positions of cards on a framework. Doing exercises with cards where it involves the use of memory may do likewise. Doing rationale diversions, for example, Sudoku, chess and crosswords can keep the brain active while acquiring new abilities.

Never believe you're excessively old, making it impossible to stay up with the latest news, and with new innovation, for example, the web, Astronomy, cellular telephones, new disclosures and so forth: adapting new aptitudes keeps new associations framing in the mind.

On the off chance that you need to keep your mind dynamic, broadly educate it with a scope of thinking undertakings, for example, Sudoku as well as tasking memory games. The mind recalls by making passionate connections. In case you're distracted, brainstorm a photo of what you need to recall, and recollect more than one issue by connecting these pictures.

In the event that your psyche is all around practiced then you are likewise going to be more resistant to life troubles. A psyche that thinks in an adjusted manner is less inclined to succumb to certain mental grievances.

The most rationally well individuals are great at managing their feelings. They tend to stay cool, instead of responding savagely with tears, outrage or trepidation. Figure out how to keep your mentality in check and you will be better furnished to adapting to life.

Keep your breathing casual and profound to help control your psyches response to occasions. When we feel on edge, our breathing frequently turns out to be speedy and shallow.

Inhale through your nose and exhale profoundly out of your stomach (not your chest). Stay physically unperturbed. Workout, hot showers and stretching are great exercises for reducing muscle strain.

Keep up an inspirational disposition when challenges are out of control by envisioning or pondering something comforting. Take a couple of minutes to envision a most loved spot, gliding in the ocean or lying in bed, and you'll switch into a more settled physical state of mind.

Chapter 15

Take 7 Key Steps to Manifest Your Dreams and Desires

Converse with many people about the power of living and their eyes will simply look over. It will be clear they are completely shut out of the thought, especially those in Western Cultures. The mere thought that your unconscious personality can have the ability to convey genuine physical things, to them appears to be silly. But even the art of quantum physics, is presently accepting the truth that this is not exactly what they initially thought.

Contemplations are a type of energy, and can be guided in approaches to have an impact on outer surroundings when concentrated effectively. The 7 stages that should be reliably taken after to completely use your oblivious personality are concisely written here.

1- Keep the end in core focus

Consistently remember yourself what accomplishing the desire will mean to your family and use. Endeavour not to lose sight of this vision and over and again concentrate on it.

2- Expect your longing will materialize

Thoroughly focusing on the thought that your longing will be delivered, by one means or another, someway will drive you forward and make you focused on your result.

3- Imagine you have what you desire at this point

Just imagine that your subconscious mind which is a powerful tool, does not know the difference between projection and reality, present or past. Use this as a guide so that your brain and entire being is being stimulated and now has whatever it desires. As a result, get your mind to trust that you now have all you wish for & that you are not lacking anything.

4- Exclude Negativity

Concentrating on the absence of something will just draw in a greater amount of the something you need. For instance, on the off chance that you wish to show a more extensive friend network then heading off to a gathering with the conviction that you are second rate compared to others is not the best outlook to be in. You will just separate yourself from the group and make you keep down from any associations, or timid far from getting included in discussions.

5- Keep Focused

You have to outrageously concentrate on the yearning you need to accomplish. Keep constantly helping yourself to remember what it will intend to you once it is a major part of your life. On the off chance that you have envisioned this effectively enough, this will give you the "fuel" or "juice" to adhere to your new conviction framework and the undertaking ahead.

6- Let the Past Go

Try not to let your old reasons for, dismissals, fear and different snags keep you down. Happenings of the past has no bearing on the future so acknowledge the obligation of moving your life in the course you wish and you will soon be showing your wishes into reality.

7- Forgive & let go

Try not to keep thinking so as to whip yourself about how others insulted you and how you will never forget. You are fairly like somebody holding another in chain and that implies you will never go anyplace unless you discharge the individual that you are holding in chain through annoyance and vengeance.

Fulfilling desires can be accomplished through the above briefly listed plan. Release yourself to the universe and it will convey all that you long for. Good fortunes and think beyond practical boundaries!

Conclusion

Your state of mind to anything is relative to the result you will achieve for whatever it is. The way you see things in life becomes a picture in your psyche and imagination and this eventually becomes the mental pictures within your energy vibration to your outer world.

The lenses through which we see life turns into the picture we see in the long run. In the event that you change your state of mind from negative to a positive mind personality, a completely different result emerges.

The force or power inside all of us controls us and our identity traits. However, once we become the master of our own thoughts and actions, that means we are already in control of this force from its root within us.

The enthusiasm to win, the drive to accomplish things in life and the perseverance to continue pushing ahead becomes easy and within our reach. When events happening outside and within our environment is making effort to influence our inner power in order to control our fate, we can see that our inner power is in control of our outer influences. At this stage, we have the full capability to define what we allow in and reject those thoughts, ideas and habits we do not wish to welcome into our lives.

Life's Cage:
Habit, Character, and Lifestyle

Life's Cage:
Thought ⇨ Deeds ⇨ Habit ⇨ Attitude ⇨ Lifestyle

Made in the USA
Charleston, SC
11 June 2016